ENLIGHTENED DESPOTISM

Reform or Reaction?

PROBLEMS IN EUROPEAN CIVILIZATION

ENLIGHTENED DESPOTISM

Reform or Reaction?

EDITED WITH AN INTRODUCTION BY

Roger Wines, FORDHAM UNIVERSITY

D. C. HEATH AND COMPANY · BOSTON

Table of Contents

I. TOWARD A DEFINITION OF
ENLIGHTENED DESPOTISM

GEORGE DUTCHER
The Importance of Enlightened Despotism   1

FRANCO VALSECCHI
A Crisis of Values   6

WALTER HUBATSCH
The Nature of Absolutism   10

IMMANUEL KANT
The Nature of Enlightenment   14

VOLTAIRE
The Philosopher-Prince   18

LEO GERSHOY
Theorists of Enlightened Despotism   20

PAUL HAZARD
The Philosophers and the Kings   24

FRITZ HARTUNG
A Definition of Enlightened Despotism   28

II. THREE ENLIGHTENED DESPOTS:
FREDERICK II, JOSEPH II, CATHERINE II

G. P. GOOCH
Frederick the *Philosophe*   32

LEO GERSHOY
A Royal Reactionary   35

FRITZ HARTUNG
The Typical Enlightened Despot   38

WILHELM TREUE
Joseph II: Enlightened Reformer   42

ERNST WANGERMANN
Joseph II: Determined by Circumstances   45

MELVIN C. WREN
Catherine as Enlightened Empress   47

R. D. CHARQUES
The Darker Side of Catherine's Reign   54

III. INTERPRETATIONS OF ENLIGHTENED DESPOTISM

CHARLES MORAZÉ
Based on Louis XIV, not Voltaire   57

GEORGES LEFEBVRE
A Compromise with Aristocracy   62

ERNST WALDER
Enlightened Despotism and the French Revolution: Similar
Goals, Different Methods   65

GEORGES LEFEBVRE
Enlightened Despotism and the French Revolution: Rejected,
yet Fulfilled   70

LEO JUST
A Foundation of Nineteenth-Century Politics   72

LEO GERSHOY
The Seed Plot of Liberalism   75

Suggestions for Additional Reading   78

Introduction

THE FIFTY YEARS before the French Revolution saw the culmination not only of the Enlightenment but also of the development of royal absolutism. In Lord Acton's phrase, it was "the monarchs' age of repentance." Never were the old monarchies so efficient, so concerned with their social and economic obligations, or with the rational pursuit of their political interests as on the eve of the uprising which declared them bankrupt by fiat of the people. Clearly there was an important relationship between the great intellectual current of the age and the political structure of Europe which contained both negative and positive aspects. To a large extent this oftimes contradictory relationship was personified in a number of monarchs, imbued with the new ideas of the Enlightenment, who tried to apply them to the perfection of their absolute rule. Thus was born enlightened despotism.

While most historians have recognized the phenomenon, they have not been in full agreement either about the nature of absolutism, its stages of development, or its precise relationship to the various conservative and liberal elements in the thought of the Enlightenment. At face value the expression "enlightened despotism" or "enlightened absolutism" would appear to be a contradiction in terms. The attempt to resolve that contradiction has spawned a special field of historical literature which this collection of readings will attempt to sample. In the eyes of later generations, the Enlightenment appeared to be a liberal movement which bequeathed to the nineteenth century the vision of constitu-

tional government and the equal rights of man. But in the eighteenth century, the reform-minded *philosophes* were surprisingly comfortable with the notion of absolute monarchy. Men like Diderot and Voltaire in France, Sonnenfels in Austria, Beccaria in Italy turned to the absolute rulers as a realistic means of attaining justice and the pursuit of happiness. A number of reasons explain why men who favored liberal principles should endorse absolutism in practice.

There was admiration for, but also mistrust in representative government, which Voltaire declared was suited chiefly for very small republics in the article on Democracy in his Philosophical Dictionary. In the social context of eighteenth-century Europe, only the superstitious mob or the privileged nobility might have gained influence in a representative government and both were targets of the *philosophes'* reform. The habit of monarchy was yet strong, and if the old aura of Divine Right had faded, along with the increasingly secularist climate of opinion, a new ideal of service to the state seemed capable of taking its place as the justification for the prince's continued existence.

"A well considered government," Frederick the Great noted in his Political Testament of 1752, "must have an underlying concept so well integrated that it could be likened to a system of philosophy. All actions must be well reasoned; finance, politics and the army must be conducted toward the same goal, the strengthening of the state and the furthering of its powers. Such a system can flow from only a single brain. It must be that of the sovereign." But such a ruler could not be either wilful or lazy: "the prince is the first servant of the state."

The chief obstacles to a thoroughgoing reform of society which would produce equality before the law and of opportunity for all classes were the corporatively organized landed nobility, urban patricians, the churches, the guilds. Only mob revolt or royal reform possessed sufficient force to break down the entrenched legal position of these adversaries. Small wonder that middle-class apostles of reason hoped for a philosopher-king who would break the position of the privileged orders from above, by reforming the laws and educating his subjects. Critics might rail at the abuses of tyranny in general, but the ruler who offered to carry out the desired reforms, the "despot légale," the "enlightened despot" could not but be praised.

Enlightened thinkers were more interested in religious and social reform than in purely political problems. The form of the state interested many of them less than its duty to educate mankind to virtue and happiness. The Baron D'Holbach stated their program: "if error and prejudice have forged the chain of the peoples, if prejudice perpetuates them, science, reason, truth, will some day break them." Another *philosophe,* Helvetius, urged that solely through good laws could virtuous men be formed. Whatever its reservations about the strong-willed rule of the enlightened despots, enlightened public opinion applauded them as the only possible way to reform.

For the *philosophes* and the kings had much to offer one another. They shared a limited range of genuine common interests: toleration, education, better justice strengthened the state as well as its subjects. The rulers derived a measure of popularity from their scholarly admirers which facilitated the introduction of measures to strengthen their states. Not only did the thinkers supply suggestions for reform; they helped to motivate the developing royal bureaucracy, and entertained the monarchs with their often fulsome flattery. On the other hand, the kings fulfilled the bargain by rationalizing the administration of government and justice, promoting more (if not complete) equality of subjects before the law, by building schools, and enlarging economic opportunity. There was some amelioration of the lot of the peasantry. Above all, the kings established toleration, curbed the power of the churches, and supported leading *philosophes* with honors and pensions. If the measures were intended more for the utility of the absolute ruler than his people, if behind the facade one glimpsed dark corners of Frederick the Great's militarism, and Catherine the Great's brutal treatment of the peasantry, one could overlook a few things. For Frenchmen, at least, how useful these eastern monarchs were; more telling than the fictitious letters of any Persian traveller, the idealized example of the enlightened despot could be used to castigate the injustices of the France of Louis XV!

Absolute monarchy was a centuries-old phenomenon; enlightened public opinion something new. The conjunction of the two reached its peak in the two decades following the Peace of Paris of 1763. In these years, as European rulers turned to the task of repairing the ravages of war upon their countries, significant innovations were made in law and government, and many of the cherished theories of the enlightened thinkers became applied fact. But by the 1780's the failure to apply enlightened despotism in France, and the success of its application elsewhere finally brought a dissatisfaction with its limitations. An absolute system of government was preferable under a good king, the Marquis D'Argenson warned, "but nature and experience demonstrate that there are ten bad ones for every good." The English historian Edward Gibbon, describing the fall of Rome, pointed out the disasters which befell the Empire after the death of its "enlightened despot," Marcus Aurelius. European intellectuals began to look beyond the sovereignty of the monarch to the ultimate sovereignty of the people. So did one of the enlightened despots, Peter Leopold of Tuscany, who went so far as to draw up a constitution with representative government for his lands.

During the ensuing years of the French Revolution, the heritage of enlightened despotism persisted, gradually changing in content. In Napoleon, according to the French historian Albert Sorel, it reached its culmination. In Germany, the era swept away clerical rule, rationalized the political boundaries, and installed enlightened reformers in the ministries of Prussia, Bavaria, and the smaller states. The French occupation remade Italy. Even after 1815, in retreat before the new forces of romantic conservatism and religious revival, aspects of enlightened absolutism lingered on until nearly mid-century in parts of Germany and Austria.

The expression "enlightened despotism" offers an interesting example of how an historical concept is coined and modified in the course of subsequent study. The idea of a "philosopher-king" goes back at least as far as Plato, and recurs frequently in the Middle Ages and the Renaissance, when there arose a special gênre of literature, the "Mirror of Princes" composed of handbooks for the instruction of such ideal monarchs. But the formulation of a specific theory of enlightened despotism could only come in the eighteenth century after the development of absolutism had put in the monarchs' hands sufficient power to force through major changes in feudal society, and when the decline of the old religious conception of monarchy necessitated a new justification based upon utility and reason. Strong-willed monarchs like Peter the Great of Russia or Frederick William I of Prussia impressed reforms upon their backward lands with great success, though neither bears much relationship to the intellectual movement which we call the Enlightenment. Their successors, Catherine II of Russia and Frederick II of Prussia followed similar policies, but

justified them with the vocabulary of the enlightenment. The latter explained, "I am a philosopher by inclination and a politician by duty."

But were the enlightened despots motivated by the enlightenment, or by the old desire of aggrandizing the power of their states? There are contradictions between their deeds and their public utterances. This has given rise to an historical debate which continues to the present day.

The expression "enlightened despotism" originated in the eighteenth century. Several of the French thinkers of the Physiocrat school spoke of a "despotisme légale" and Diderot used the term "despotisme eclairée" in his letters. Serious historical discussion of the term came much later. In 1874 the German economist Wilhelm Röscher attempted to explain the development of the European absolute monarchy by positing three stages. The first, a "confessional absolutism" of the sixteenth century, was based on the idea "cuius regio, eius religio" and embodied in the Spanish King Philip II. Then followed a "courtly absolutism" exemplified by Louis XIV and "L'etat c'est moi." Finally, the eighteenth century produced "enlightened absolutism" of which Frederick the Great was the chief advocate, describing himself as "the first servant of the state."

Frederick's great biographer Reinhold Koser took issue with Röscher's categories, insisting in 1889 that stages of absolutism could only be derived from a concrete study of the inner development of the machinery of royal government, not from ideology. He distinguished between the still incomplete absolutism of the Renaissance and the "thorough" absolutism of Louis XIV's France. To Koser, the enlightened despotism of the eighteenth century marked a decline, a retreat from the unlimited power of the crown, which now had to answer to enlightened public opinion.

By the time of the First World War, researches in several countries had generated much new evidence on absolutism, while scholars became more interested in intellectual trends and began to question the influence which enlightened thought had upon eighteenth-century monarchy. In 1928, when historians gathered in Oslo for an International Congress of the Historical Sciences, Professor M. L'Heritier of France complained about the "vague and confused" state of knowledge about enlightened despotism. He called for an international committee of scholars to study jointly the phenomenon in the various European states. This interesting experiment in cooperative historical research bore considerable fruit. Despite the reluctance of some historians to take part (the English insisted that they had never been governed by despotism and abstained from the committee), several reports outlining the history of enlightened despotism in the continental states were published in the Bulletin of the International Committee of the Historical Sciences. Leo Gershoy's selection in this book skilfully synthesizes much of this material.

The discussion was continued by Fritz Hartung, the dean of German constitutional historians, who took a leading part in the international committee. He took issue with the earlier work of Röscher and Koser, and rejected the suggestion of L'Heritier that the term be applied to ancient rulers, non-western potentates, or post-1789 figures like Napoleon I. Instead, he urged that a precise usage of the phrase "enlightened absolutism" be adopted to characterize the effects of the European Enlightenment upon the specifically European type of absolute monarchy. For Hartung, Frederick the Great marked the epitome of enlightened absolutism; with him absolutism reached the culmination of a centuries-long development: "the achievements of Frederick are undeniable, but also the judgement that with him absolutism had fulfilled its task." The Prussian ruler stood not at the threshold of a new liberal era, but at the end of a long line of kings.

Since the 1930's the intellectual and social world of the eighteenth century has

attracted many historians. Paul Hazard and Alfred Cobban have sketched the transformation of the European mind. Hazard's selection in this book indicates his skepticism of the extent to which the despots were personally enlightened. Cobban went so far in his *In Search of Humanity* as to dismiss the concept of "enlightened despotism" as a useless "textbook category." He insisted upon the fundamentally libertarian nature of the Enlightenment, which was incompatible with despotism. In the same vein, J. O. Lindsay managed to write a skilful chapter on eighteenth-century royal government for Volume VII of the *New Cambridge Modern History* without even mentioning the term. But whatever the hesitations of English writers, continental historians continue to work within the framework and terminology of enlightened absolutism.

The postwar years have seen new investigations of the economic and social basis of the *ancien régime*. Seen in an Atlantic context by Robert R. Palmer, enlightened despotism appeared as a last futile attempt to preserve royal power in the face of a world-wide democratic revolution. Georges Lefebvre pointed out that it was an attempt to translate modern western practices to underdeveloped eastern Europe. Charles Morazé suggested that the fiscal practices of England and the example of Louis XIV were more important factors in the despots' governing than the ideas of Voltaire. Ernst Walder showed how enlightened despotism shared many of the same goals as the French Revolution, but was unable to satisfy the middle classes because of its authoritarian rule. In the final selection used in this book, Leo Gershoy analyzed and interpreted the contradictory legacy, and affirmed the positive and liberal heritage of the age of enlightened despots.

In the following excerpts, the editor has tried to give the reader an introduction to the continuing debate over the nature and effects of enlightened despotism. The material is widely scattered and many of the larger works, especially the biographies, do not lend themselves easily to excerpting, so that the student is advised to read further along the lines suggested at the end of this book. Again, the editor has attempted to emphasize more recent studies, although many of the older articles are still quite relevant and useful.

The first section inquires into the nature of enlightened despotism, the extent to which it was enlightened, and to which it was absolute. After this attempt at clarification and definition, there follows a sampling of material on three of the most famous despots, Frederick the Great of Prussia, Catherine the Great of Russia, and Joseph II of Austria. The concluding section discusses the significance of enlightened despotism in the light of recent historical research.

Though a substantial verdict is in, historians continue to debate the nature of eighteenth-century thought and government. Was enlightened despotism a genuine reform movement, motivated by the Enlightenment, or an attempt by the monarchs to cling to their power in an age of change? Did it mark a culmination or a decline in the development of absolutism? Was it a new and advanced political movement, or merely the application of seventeenth-century methods to the backward areas of eighteenth-century Europe? Was it ephemeral, or did it produce any lasting effects? Did this contradictory combination of philosophy and politics provide a constructive alternative to the French Revolution? Were the kings using the philosophers, or the philosophers using the kings? In short, was enlightened despotism reaction or reform?

[NOTE: Footnotes have been omitted in the following selections, and some deletions have been made, in order to conserve space. Readers are referred to the original works for full text and documentation.]

The Conflict of Opinion

I. Toward a definition:

"The new enlightened thought was grafted on to the old trunk of dynastic absolutism. . . . The centralization of the state, pursued for centuries, reached its crowning point. . . . The enlightenment with its contract theory and its egalitarian premises freed the state from the system of privilege and allowed the unconditional assertion of its powers."

— Franco Valsecchi

"The power of the rulers was absolute . . . but the supposedly absolute ruler of the Baroque age was still a long distance from the absolutism of the modern democratic state . . ."

— Walther Hubatsch

". . . These champions of enlightened despotism dwelt in a strange political no-man's-land, a border country still reminiscent of old regime absolutism, but verging upon the new terrain of parliamentary constitutionalism. . . . Resigning their children and grandchildren to the seeming tranquillity of a world without princes, they made the best of the present world by keeping the prince on his throne, but on leading strings of purple . . ."

— Leo Gershoy

"The philosophers thought that they were using the kings, and it was the kings who were using them."

— Paul Hazard

"I would characterize enlightened absolutism as a form of government strongly influenced by philosophy, especially the political philosophy of the enlightenment."

— Fritz Hartung

II. The enlightened despots:

"Of the three leading enlightened autocrats of the eighteenth century, Frederick the Great was the earliest and the most significant. If anyone did, he certainly embodied Plato's philosophical king, who interested himself equally in power politics and intellectual questions. . . . The "alte Fritz" was the first and only *philosophe,* historian, political theoretician, poet and musician from the House of Hohenzollern. . . ."

— G. P. Gooch

"The dynamic ruler was . . . a reforming reactionary who propounded solutions for the dilemmas of a new age in terms of remedies that were already outmoded for his own."

— Leo Gershoy

". . . When Maria Theresa died in 1780, her oldest son . . . Joseph II was almost forty. Now he had the possibility to realize his reform ideas, which belonged entirely to the enlightenment. . . . His conviction, that life could and should be controlled completely by the state, according to reason and utility, led to many failures . . ."

— Wilhelm Treue

"A policy of enlightened despotism thus appeared in Austria no less than elsewhere in response to certain practical and urgent necessities and not as the fruit of philosophical persuasion. . . . The 'revolutionary' emperor undertook little that was entirely new in principle."

— Ernst Wangermann

III. The effects of enlightened despotism:

"No reform in Europe was due to the thought of the *philosophes*. . . . Nothing in the real or concrete institutions of Europe owed anything to the France of the eighteenth century; they owed almost everything to the France of the seventeenth century."

— Charles Morazé

"The reforms of enlightened despotism helped to awaken the non-privileged classes in the Habsburg dominions from their political slumber and to bring them, for the first time since the Reformation, into the field of political action. Not all the consequences of such a political renaissance had, however, been foreseen by Joseph II, and some of them alarmed him and his successors acutely."

— Ernst Wangermann

"In Germany absolutism did not end with Frederick II of Prussia nor with the French Revolution. . . . The long duration of absolutism in Germany influenced the character of the nation so that it developed very late [a] sense of individual civic responsibility . . ."

— Leo Just

"Much that our age holds dear was manifestly served by the triumph of an enlightened despotism whose ultimate ends were realized through revolutionary means in 1789. Its deeply embedded humanist and humanitarian liberalism was subsequently fused with and "corrected" by the less ingenuous economic liberalism of nineteenth-century free enterprise; but together they eventuated in parliamentary democracy, utilitarian ethics, classical economics, and the Concert of Europe."

— Leo Gershoy

I. TOWARD A DEFINITION OF ENLIGHTENED DESPOTISM

The Importance of Enlightened Despotism

GEORGE DUTCHER

George M. Dutcher (1874–1959) was a long-time professor of English history and a vice-president of Cornell University. He edited the 1931 edition of the *Guide to Historical Literature*. In this selection, which is taken from the 1920 *Annual Report* of the American Historical Association, he summarizes the state of scholarship on enlightened despotism at the beginning of the decade which was to show great interest and much further investigation in the topic. Dutcher emphasizes the priority of practical over theoretical considerations in forming the policies of the despots and raises several of the issues debated by later scholars.

THE MOST important development in governmental practice on the continent of Europe in the eighteenth century prior to the outbreak of the French Revolution was the enlightened despotism. This movement has sometimes been miscalled the benevolent despotism by those who emphasize certain of the humanitarian reforms which characterized it, without considering the circumstances and motives which lay back of these reforms. In fact, so far as I am aware, writers have hitherto confined their attention to registering certain acts of the enlightened despotism without attempting to analyze that manifestation.

The element which was new in enlightened despotism was not despotism but enlightenment. The word "enlightenment" as used in this connection, as well as its German equivalent *Aufklaerung* signified in a very definite sense rationalism, or more correctly, the recognition of the authority of reason. The philosophical eighteenth century rejected divine right as the foundation of the state in favor of reason — enlightenment as the basic authority. Enlightenment, in this sense, while primarily an intellectual movement, found practical application in the fields of both religion and government. In the field of religion it expressed the reaction against mysticism and pietism. It was represented in England by the Deistic school culminating in Bolingbroke and Hume; in France by Voltaire and the Encyclopedists; in Germany most distinctively by Wolff. This movement did not necessarily limit itself to the ideas propounded by the Deistic group but included various forms of refusal to submit to authority in matters of church and of personal religion. In the relations of state and church it signified the supremacy of the state in all matters not clearly of a spiritual character. In this respect the movement culminated in the suppression of the Society of Jesus in the Catholic lands.

On the side of government the problem

From George Dutcher, "This Enlightened Despotism: Reform or Reaction?" *Annual Report of the American Historical Association* (1920), pp. 189–190, 191–193. Reprinted by permission of the American Historical Association.

appeared in its simplest form in England where the conditions, arising after the Restoration and centering in the Revolution of 1688, developed the theories of non-resistance and of passive obedience. The significance of these theories, which are so puzzling to the present-day mind, is that out of the conflict between king and parliament there came the recognition of the supremacy of the state quite apart from any individual, even though that individual were the monarch. Even the extreme Tory, Bolingbroke, recognized as the one valid aim the union of all in the service of the state, though he looked to the "patriotic king," not to parliament for leadership in that union.

In France the development of the movement prior to the Revolution was very largely on the theoretical rather than the practical side, and nowhere was the discussion so broad in its scope or carried with clearer conviction to its logical conclusions. In Germany the result was the reverse of that in England. There, too, the logical development was a recognition of the supremacy of the state, but owing to the lack of properly developed self-governing institutions the leadership of the state was without question vested in the monarch. In Germany too, thanks to Wolff, the frank and full application of the rationalistic principles to the state was most clearly set forth, and, thanks to the practical genius as well as the philosophical instinct of Frederick the Great, it received its most complete demonstration in the enlightened despotism of that prince.

In matters of government the enlightened despotism operated primarily in three fields. The first was in the development of law as a natural correlative to the supremacy of the state. This involved the development of uniformity of law and the consequent movement toward codification, to which Frederick gave particular attention. The second phase was in the tendency toward equality before the law, both of territorial areas and of classes of the population. This movement looked toward centralization and uniformity in administration, and toward the minimizing, if not the abolition, of privilege. The third field was that of administrative efficiency which involved the development of systematic administration, as increased powers came with the progress of centralization of authority. Administration had to respond to the demands and tests of reason by seeing that the government produced for the state the goods which reason approved, especially in matters diplomatic, military, financial, and economic. The characteristic form of administrative system thus developed was bureaucracy. After this brief and inadequate survey or analysis of the enlightened despotism, it is my purpose to undertake to trace not the development of theory, but the practical working out of events which culminated in the enlightened despotism of Frederick the Great and Maria Theresa and to show how Prussia and Austria, rather than the more advanced nations, England and France, became the birthplace of the enlightened despotism. . . .

In England it naturally came to pass that, after the elimination of feudal privilege in the Wars of the Roses and of ecclesiastical privilege in the Reformation, the commons were able to wage uncomplicated and effective war on royal prerogative in the great Civil War and the Revolution of 1688, and to enter the eighteenth century with England fully and clearly organized as a constitutional monarchy, thoroughly unified and nationalized to participate in the struggle for world empire. Neither royalty nor nobility nor clergy but the commonalty of the realm won for England the splendid triumph sealed by the peace of Paris in 1763.

With this development in England there stand in contrast the contemporary changes and results in France and in the lands on which rested the shadow rather than the yoke of the Holy Roman Empire.

France, in the fifteenth century, emerged victorious from its Hundred Years' War with England and triumphant in the efforts of the royal power against the forces of feudal provincialism; but, without awaiting the completion of the task of national consolidation, plunged rashly into wars of conquest in Italy and of rivalry with Charles V. Ere those wars were ended the Reformation had come to add ecclesiastical strife and afford the restless nobility an opportunity, through the civil wars of religion, to undermine the royal authority and recover political power for their selfish advantage. Henry IV asserted the principles of religious toleration and of the supremacy of national interests and authority, in order that he and his successors might give themselves to the task of humbling the feudal nobility and of exalting the royal power. The double success of Mazarin in the treaties of Westphalia and in compassing the collapse of the Fronde assured the triumph of the royal power and of nationalism, but did not involve the annihilation or even decimation of the feudal nobility, or the abolition or diminution of their privileges. The nobility and the clergy alike were compelled to accept the royal authority and to find their grandeur no longer in their own glory but in reflecting the splendor of royalty. The royal power in France was built upon substantial geographical, racial, and linguistic unity and upon an historical tradition of success and of realization of national ambitions. In contrast with England, however, royalty alone, in France, reaped the political fruits of the victory of the alliance of king and people against the nobility, for the states-general failed to develop from a feudal into a popular representative body or into an effective governmental institution, and from 1614 onward really ceased to exist.

In France, therefore, the royal power became the sole institutional expression of the unity, aims, and action of the nation. It was absolute in the field and its field was the best in Europe. In 1660 no state on the European continent could compare with France in its territorial compactness and its advantageous geographical situation, or in the homogeneity of its population and the solidarity and efficiency of its governmental system, or in the extent and exploitation of its economic resources.

The French monarchy of Louis XIV could readily command unquestioning national support in the twofold ambition of securing national strategic frontiers and of achieving the paramountcy in the European system and hence the leadership in world empire. Monarchy in France faced no opposition, was confronted by no political institutions or moral authority or compelling necessity that would hold it to account.

The output of the French mind on political, social, and economic questions in the 15 years beginning with the publication in 1748 of Montesquieu's Spirit of the Laws, and culminating in 1762 in the appearance of Rousseau's Social Contract, was destined not merely to compass the downfall of the French monarchy but to remake the political life of Europe. In those very years when France was formulating the thought of the coming age, two monarchs, the Prussian and the Austrian, were developing policies of efficiency in monarchical administration because war had taught them its necessity in the struggle for existence and for empire.

While it is notorious that the two most intelligent and progressive countries, England and France, did not exemplify the enlightened despotism, that movement had its home and did its most notable work in the lands nominally comprised in the Holy Roman Empire.

Frederick II was first of these Hohenzollerns with the genius and daring for aggressive measures. In his first and second Silesian wars he risked the whole achievement of three generations on the chance of a conspicuous conquest, and won, as much by his ruthless diplomacy as by military ability.

None the less this experience confirmed Frederick in the Hohenzollern conception of the state and of the methods of its enhancement. He realized that the life and growth of the state were dependent upon the maintenance of an effective military machine, which in turn could be maintained and operated only with large and readily available financial power, which could alone be drawn from the fullest exploitation of the state's economic resources by the steady hard work of its subjects.

The ten years' truce which followed the treaty of Dresden (1745) might be described as the adolescent period of the enlightened despotism. It still awaits proper study from this point of view, which is more important than the diplomatic one which has customarily held the attention. While Frederick devoted himself unremittingly during this interval to the improvement of his army and finances and to the development of the economic resources of his dominions, his defeated opponent, Maria Theresa, was not blind to the lessons of defeat and set herself likewise with indefatigable earnestness to achieve in similar ways such results for Austria that the struggle might be renewed, the lost provinces retrieved, and the national honor redeemed.

In his task Frederick conceived of himself as the first servant of the state. Unlike the Bourbon who could identify himself with the state, the Hohenzollern had been forced to conceive of the state as an entity apart from himself or his subjects though including them. The state was something above persons and more permanent and enduring than individuals. Such a concept could scarcely have been developed in England or France, while it was not an unnatural adaptation from the theory of the universal and paramount state which, rather than any concrete realization thereof, had subsisted for centuries as the Holy Roman Empire.

It appears, therefore, that the first efforts to practice as a deliberate policy the basic principles of the enlightened despotism began prior to the appearance of any of the important French writings mentioned previously and had been interrupted by the Seven Years' War before some of the more

significant of them had appeared. This earliest phase of enlightened despotism was, then, little more than two parallel national campaigns of preparedness in two rival states, between two rival dynasties, in anticipation of a desperate military struggle for leadership within the German lands. On either side the purpose was the strengthening and girding of the state for aggrandizement; on the one hand to hold a recently captured province, on the other to recover that lost province, which each regarded as the key to the situation. Each side considered that the outcome of the struggle would be determined by the effectiveness of the marshaling of the resources of the state in support of its military program. The results justified the policy, for Frederick's own efforts retained the province which the consistent policy of his predecessors had made it possible for him to seize and it left him in the position of primacy in Germany. On the other hand, while Maria Theresa failed in these purposes, she emerged from the struggle with her powers greatly strengthened in her remaining dominions and in a position to recoup military losses in Germany through political gains in Italy and Poland.

It is also important to note that in both cases the monarch was dealing with lands devoid of geographic unity and awkwardly situated so that they lacked the natural and strategic frontiers which, in whole or in large measure, characterized England and France. Military power was essential to offset the lack of nature's gifts, in which matter Prussia labored under the more serious handicap. Furthermore, neither state could compare with England or France in the racial and linguistic homogeneity of its population, though in this respect the handicap of Austria was the more serious. In still other matters both states were at serious disadvantage as compared with England and France. Neither could enjoy the advantage of a compact and harmoniously developed and organized political system, for geography denied it to

Prussia and race withheld it from Austria. Nor could either utilize the priceless heritage of historic solidarity with a venerable record of national cooperation in enduring severe tests and effecting glorious achievements which constitutes such powerful challenge to each new generation to maintain the honor of the national name and the security of the national estate. Then, again, neither Frederick nor Maria Theresa could rely upon their prestige, whether as individuals or as the hereditary chiefs of their respective dynasties, to rally their subjects to their support.

In each case, therefore, the consolidation of subjects and resources had to be achieved by other means. Policy must serve where nature and history failed. It was impossible to bide the time which should prove to each province and people its better welfare and larger opportunity within the state to which it happened to belong than might be its lot in any other possible state. The monarch must prejudge such decision and act for himself and his subjects on the assumed truth of such conclusion. He must not leave the question open to the slightest doubt; he must think and plan and act for himself and his subjects, and compel his subjects to cooperate in action without thinking. It was not the part of the subject to think, but only to obey as if under martial law. Popular or constitutional government was impossible of consideration. Neither the church nor feudalism could be relied upon as voluntary of self-convinced associates, for apparent self-interest might readily lead them to other conclusions. Despotism was the only possible solution, and it must follow a policy so obviously reasonable — enlightened — that it should not arouse any doubts but should secure, with a minimum of friction or delay, the maximum result.

Neither the monarch nor the monarchy, but the state, was the ultimate entity to which all else must be subordinate. The state was an utterly intangible and unembodiable thing but none the less extremely real. It was that policy which comprehended the necessities and ideals whose attainment bound sovereign and subjects alike to service for their realization as the absolute general welfare for the present and even more for the future. For the attainment of the ends of the state, coin or commodity, toil or life were alike things to be expended with frugality or with abandon, as circumstances might require. No benevolent sentiment or humane motive, but sheer cold reason — enlightenment, was to determine the methods to be pursued, or was to be considered as an end for which the state existed, though humanitarianism might very possibly chance to be incidental to both methods and aims. The ends sought were the permanency, security, and aggrandizement of the state, for these were the sole safeguards in the struggle for existence which lands and peoples so situated as Prussia and Austria have ever felt compelled to seek.

In conclusion, I can only emphasize the priority in the development of the policies of Frederick the Great and Maria Theresa to the appearance of the great creative writings of the French political and economic thinkers to whom has customarily been ascribed the initiative for the enlightened despotism. The exaltation of the state rather than of the monarch, the undermining of provincial rights and class privileges, the effort to secure uniformity in the incidence of governmental authority, the demand on the administrative system for efficiency, the efforts for codification of law and the reform of the judicial system, the aggressive instead of intriguing diplomacy, the most comprehensive demands for military service, the improved military organization, the more thorough systematization of the finances, the fuller recognition that government finances are dependent upon sound economic conditions — these all appeared in Frederick's policy in the first decade of his reign and were promptly copied with more or less success by Maria Theresa. On the religious side, the enlightenment was a personal, scarcely a governmental, interest with Frederick, and altogether abhorrent to Maria Theresa. It was only with Joseph II that this element developed as not merely a personal interest but also as a wide-reaching governmental policy. . . .

A Crisis of Values

FRANCO VALSECCHI

Franco Valsecchi (1903–   ) a professor of history at Milan, is one of the leading historians of the age of enlightenment, and a special expert on Italian history of the period. He is the author of several works, including his two volume *l'Assolutismo illustrato in Austria e in Lombardia*. The following selection emphasizes the intellectual roots of enlightened governmental theory, and relates it to the fiscal crisis which absolute monarchy faced in the early eighteenth century.

THE *ancien régime,* the political, economic and social system which originated in the middle ages, entered into its decisive crisis in the first half of the eighteenth century. Dynastic absolutism succeeded, in the course of the century, in reaffirming the idea of the state as embodied in the [person of] the monarch.

The state was identified with the monarch, and conceived of as an object which was the personal possession of the sovereign, which he could dispose of like any of his property. Invested with his office by the grace of God, the prince was the source of all law, the holder of all powers. The concept of sovereignty was summed up in the formula "A Deo rex, a rege lex"; the king belongs to God, the laws belong to the king. There were, it is true, bodies, classes and institutions in the state which exercised public powers, but their prerogatives had come to be considered as a grant of the prince, not innate rights, but privileges given by the sovereign. These particular forces, whether they were those of the feudal hierarchy or of the autonomous towns, only survived as a reflection of the authority of the sovereign, and their resources were constantly diminished by invasions of the royal power, which sought to limit their field of action and repress them little by little.

Nonetheless, no matter how much their submission was completed, the forces of particularism did not cease to exist. The social and juridical system inherited from the middle ages remained, as did the hierarchy of classes based on privilege, the feudal prerogatives, ecclesiastical immunities and the autonomous towns. The whole network of particular powers impeded the exercise of royal authority, dividing the power of the state into fragments. No one could legislate uniformly for an [entire] country. The authority of the monarch extended over all his dominions, but assumed different aspects in each of them, always respecting local privileges, institutions and traditions. Everyone lived under his own laws, rather than those of the king, and thereby limited the apparent omnipotence of the sovereign.

From Franco Valsecchi, *Storia D'Italia,* Vol. VII (Milan, 1959), pp. 537–545. Used by permission of Arnaldo Mondadori Editore. Translated by the editor.

The need of absolute government to unify and centralize was fulfilled by an affirmation of the central power, not by a removal of the old social and political structure. Absolutism had erected its own edifice upon medieval foundations, and remained bound to a past from which it was not able to free itself. Its own evolution was thus deadlocked. The survival of the regime of privilege prevented the monarchs from carrying out their historic task, the formation of a strong centralized state. . . . Beneath the apparent splendor of the monarchy the burdening problem of finances [was] a nightmare. The arbitrary distribution of financial burdens, and the no less arbitrary system of collecting and administering of debts cut sharply into income, which was more and more insufficient to meet the expenses. The grand politics of hegemony, the parasitism of the courts, devoured the resources of the most powerful dynasties of Europe in a growing, fearful deficit. In the first decades of the eighteenth century, there was not a state in Europe, large or small, which did not find itself in a situation verging upon bankruptcy. The remedies which governments adopted in order to ward off financial pressures, such as giving away the income of the state, or increasing the public debt, only aggravated the evils which they had to face.

In overcoming this deadlock which had arrested the evolution of absolutism, repair work would not suffice to meet the emergency; the entire system would have to be transformed. "In order to erect a new building, it is necessary to tear down the old." These were the words of an imperial minister, Kaunitz, the chancellor of Maria Theresa and Joseph II. His words expressed the program of a new absolutism. It proposed not to reform, but to build anew. Its first task was to demolish the edifice of the past and erect upon its foundations its own new construction upon the ruins. Thus it became the antithesis of all which preceded it. . . .

. . . The thought of the century became increasingly aware of this emergency as it asserted the great intellectual movement of the Enlightenment. The roots of [the movement] were thrust back into the Renaissance and the Reformation, while its branches had flourished with the scientific discoveries of Galileo, Newton and Kepler, along with the philosophic systems of Bacon, Leibniz and Descartes. Nature, reason, and knowledge derived from experience were its formula, and it battered against the ramparts of the old world of authority and tradition. The eighteenth century took up its ideas and transferred them from the heights of science and philosophy to the level plain of popularization, applying its terms to everyday life . . .

The movement had its beginnings in England, England which provided a whole series of innovators, from Locke to Shaftesbury to Hume. But the great work of popularization was done by France, where the material and moral crisis of the *ancien régime* reached its culminating point. The French Enlightenment derived its origins from English thought, drew its own conclusions, and moved toward the intellectual conquest of Europe. [The Enlightenment], changed into small coin by the Encyclopedia, was carried into contact with the general public. . . . Arming itself against the old regime with the mordant irony of Voltaire, interpreting the hopes of a new social order with the . . . sentimentality of Rousseau, it also suggested the laws of a new system of politics in the architectural intellectual constructions of Montesquieu.

The innovating power of [the Enlightenment] consisted in its uncompromising rejection of traditional values upon which the constitutional order was based. The Enlightenment set itself up in judgment upon the past, opposing tradition with its new tradition, named reason, which was the discovery of the new philosophy. How far reason would have gone to enlighten the world, they thought and believed, if history had not led it into a blind alley . . .

Their new world was not to be the blind world of yesterday, but a world illumined and guided by reason. Illumination, light, enlightening — these were the words which were repeated in all their writings with ever greater persuasiveness and energy. The century called itself the century of light . . . Along with this word, another is occasionally found, progress . . . The Enlightenment believed in progress without limit; the path of humanity itself was nothing less than the progressive pathway of reason.

The century of light regarded itself as the beginning of a new era in which men would learn to measure reality according to an infallible rule, whereby men would turn from error . . . "In our century," Voltaire remarked, "men have acquired more enlightenment from one part of Europe to the other, than in all the preceding ages." There still remained the sad task of liquidating the past. "Abuses take the place of law in nearly every land, and if the wisest men were to assemble to make the laws, where is the state that would remain wholly unchanged? . . ."

. . . There took place a radical revision of all values. Nor could religion escape; the century had its own faith, the faith of reason . . . An attack unleashed itself especially against the Catholic Church, the citadel of the authority and tradition which reason opposed. Along with the Church, the offensive came to attack the very intellectual foundations of the *ancien régime*. It denied the principles of divine right upon which the political and social order rested.

Thus the new thought entered as a profoundly subversive element into the conception of state and society. According to the traditional concept, the rights which the state recognized in the individual were based upon a grant from on high, from the sovereign. They were privileges bestowed, not rights belonging to the individual as such and . . . based on his nature as a human being. Enlightened thought proclaimed the unalterable value of such fundamental rights, which were to be recognized by all as the foundation of the state. The individual came to be placed at the

base of the order of the state; it was from him that the state derived its life; from him that the sovereign received his powers.

This was . . . not so much a profound change but an overthrow of the concept of sovereignty. The divine right of the prince was put aside and the origins of his power were now traced to a contract by which the people committed their sovereignty to him. . . . The contractual theory of the origin of the state . . . was an undisputed truth to all the precursors and adherents of enlightenment, from Grotius to Hobbes, from Locke to Rousseau. The traditional terms of political expression were reversed; no longer did the individual exist for the state, rather, the state for the individual. Since the sovereign was the delegate of the people, not a lord placed over them by God, he had to seek their interests and not his own. . . .

Enlightened despotism was thus a theory which contained the seeds of future political development, but which in the dynastic climate of the eighteenth century became a new impulse toward the further development of absolutism. . . . It drew upon the initial premise that sovereignty had its origins from the people . . . and concluded that its end was the benefit of the people. Sovereignty was unlimited and irrevocable. Before the rulers, the idea was espoused by the German representatives of the natural law school: Pufendorf, Thomasius, Christian Wolff. They stressed these two principles: the absolute power of the sovereign, the welfare of the people. The people had delegated their authority to the ruler in order to achieve their own improvement. The alienation of powers had to be without reserve, if they wanted the sovereign to be capable of carrying out his task. . . . He had all the rights, because he had all the duties. He was placed above the laws, but bound by a moral duty which required him to respect the fundamental rights of his subjects.

The French school . . . of the Physiocrats [taught] a formula more in harmony with the spirit of enlightenment, and resting more upon rational than upon moral values. They contrasted the political practice of "despotisme légale" with that of "arbitrary despotism." This was a distinction between the traditional concept of absolutism and the new enlightened concept. Absolutism, according to Mercier de la Rivière, the chief exponent of these ideas, was the best form of government because it contained within itself its own guarantee. The sovereign could be compared to a proprietor who managed his belongings; his own interests lay in administering it in the best manner. Absolutism guaranteed good government because the prince had every profit from governing well, every loss from governing badly.

But this presupposed one condition: that the sovereign know his proper interests, that he be conscious of his limitations, that he be, in a word, "enlightened." The basic order of society rested upon certain natural principles . . . An enlightened ruler would be one who based his actions upon such principles . . . and was aware of the true laws of nature and of reason. The guarantee consisted in the coincidence of the interest of both sovereign and subjects, which was obedience to these supreme laws. With the doctrine of legal despotism, the elements of the new absolutism were well launched on their course. . . .

The new enlightened thought was grafted onto the old trunk of dynastic absolutism . . . reinforcing it and giving it new vigor. . . . Authority demanded and justified an unlimited exercise of power, for no force had the right to oppose powers which were being exercised in the name of the common good. The forces of particularism, with their privileges and opposition to the full exercise of state power, were put in their place and made subject to common laws. The centralization of the state, which had been pursued for centuries, thus reached a crowning point. The *ancien régime,* with its privileged social hierarchy had placed an impassable barrier in the way of centralization. The Enlightenment, with its contract theory and its egalitarian premises, freed the state from the system of privilege and allowed the unconditional assertion of its powers. . . . The state's officials penetrated into the carefully guarded field of feudal rights. They proposed as the final step of reform the abolition of the chains which bound the subjects to their lords. The clergy, which had come to constitute a state within a state . . . was made subject to an implacable state surveillance which controlled and nullified the bonds which united them to Rome. It was a political battle against the ecclesiastical powers which derived its nourishment from the intellectual battle against the Catholic tradition. . . . Enlightenment and absolutism thus fought side by side and sometimes exchanged their weapons.

The rise of absolutism not only resulted in an assertion, but even in an extension of the state's powers . . . The power of the state gained not only in intensity but also in breadth . . . and its work multiplied. According to the new school of politics, the state not only had to direct political life, but also the social, economic, and spiritual life of the country. It was to take care of the material welfare of the subject as well as his moral welfare; to assure his means of life, promote productivity, supervise education, direct culture, provide for public health, and even control the growth of its population . . . Thus the tutelage over the rights of the citizen resulted in a more rigorous and invading absolutism. The idea of public happiness justified an intervention which knew no practical limits.

The subject, deprived of the right to live or die, was supposed to receive all things from the hands of the government. Frederick II of Prussia, one of the enlightened despots who was taken as a model by his century, spoke of treating his people as one treats a sick child. The machinery of state, which had been encumbered by the . . . incongruities of the old regime, was subjected to a systematic revision to meet new demands and new principles . . . clearing away the barriers of privilege, and opening the way to a solution of former problems which the *ancien régime* should have met. The administration of justice and taxes, the reef which threatened to wreck the traditional ship of state, was able to adopt a system corresponding to the rational standards of the century and to perform the tasks which it was called upon to do. . . . The rational administration of the modern state was born.

Thus absolutism, which appeared at the start of the century to have exhausted its possibilities of development, recovered its impetus and vigor. . . . The Enlighten-

ment by renewing the fundamental conception of state and society cleared the path of obstacles. The evolution of absolutism collided with the political and social inheritance of the middle ages, and the regime of privilege which had paralyzed its actions. . . . With the Enlightenment the state completed its definitive renunciation of the middle ages. Like a river which sweeps all before it, absolutism followed its course and in a few years crowned the work pursued through centuries of conflict.

The Nature of Absolutism

WALTHER HUBATSCH

Walther Hubatsch (1915–   ) has written on several periods of German history, ranging in his interests from the sixteenth-century Teutonic Knights to the twentieth-century German Navy. Currently a professor of history at Bonn University, he is best known for his work on Prussian history. The selection here is taken from a work surveying the age of absolutism. It discusses the nature of absolutism in terms of theory and practice, and compares its development in the several European states. Hubatsch points out the limitations which restricted even the most absolute of monarchs.

THE POLITICAL DOCTRINES of modern absolutism derive from Jean Bodin. In his work *De Republica* of 1576 he defined the majesty of the king as "the whole of the powers which are free of the laws to which the citizens are subject." These demands arose from the complete disorder of the sixteenth-century French political system, with its weakness, religious war and persecutions by the Church. Bodin sought to introduce . . . royal absolutism as a remedy against internal and foreign dangers. The royal sovereignty was described by him as a power "indivisible and free of any restriction." To be sure, the royal power was not entirely unlimited; the king

would become a tyrant if he put aside the natural and the divine law and made the subjects into "slaves." Though the age saw a continual interchange of ideas and actual practices in considerable confusion, and though there was opposition to these ideas from the camp of the *Monarchomachen,* absolute sovereignty prevailed, and to it France owed her recovery from the depths of ruin.

The origin of this modern phenomenon of absolutism was essentially different in the European countries and its outward forms were correspondingly quite diverse. We may disregard the Ottoman form of despotism here, but the western European

From Walther Hubatsch, *Das Zeitalter des Absolutismus* (Braunschweig, 1962), pp. 5–10. Used by permission of Professor Walther Hubatsch and Georg Westermann Verlag. Translation by the editor.

states also displayed a good deal of divergence from one another. Spain was directed by its overseas empire in the two Indies toward a rigidly centralized administration. The justification of the modern French state arose as a measure of self-survival in the middle of a religious conflict which made an ordering hand necessary. These efforts to carry out the state's task of keeping order liberated themselves from other restraints, making it possible for the desired measures to take place. The modern bureaucratic state secularized itself along with the process by which it became rationalized. The system of a mercantilistic state economy, the maintenance of a standing army even in peacetime, the division of functions within the state among specialized civil servants, were the means which were used to successfully force the old feudal state into hopeless subjection. The feudal aristocracy was excluded from politics, but continued to enjoy their social privileges, and they remained at the service of the entire state. Seventeenth-century France saw the achievement of Bodin's doctrines, which were put into practice by Richelieu. In his Political Testament, Richelieu recognized the conception of the sovereignty of the monarch, whom he likened to the representative of God.

The power of the crown was still regarded as a personal prerogative, and the life of the court conceived as an enjoyment of position and life. The sense of "plaisir de gouverner" developed under the successors of Louis XIV into "amusement" as the measure of the reality of life became lost. The formula "King by the Grace of God" which was originally an expression of humility, gradually changed along with the religious values, until it became an arrogant absolutism, in which the kings saw themselves as subject only to God.

The power of the absolute monarchy rested on the army, the church and the bureaucracy. The modern army appeared in the form of the *miles perpetuus,* and from the time of Richelieu received a modern organization, including reserve forces. Officers were now appointed by the king, and were no longer capitalist military adventurers like the *condottieri,* or the leaders of the old mercenaries. Alongside the officials of the parliaments, and alongside the clerks of the local councils, there appeared the bureaucrats of the royal administration. The new type of the *intendant* as plenipotentiary representative of the monarch became the characteristic administrator. The central organs of government were to be found at the court of the king, and they were increasingly filled with educated and professional bureaucrats. The separation of government functions was carried out much sooner in France than Prussia, which acquired this modernization for the first time after 1807. Since the French kings had exercised . . . an undisputed right of appointing their bishops since the Concordat of 1516, it became possible for them to establish a Gallican form of national church which contributed greatly to the inner strengthening of the state. Army, bureaucracy, and state religion formed the absolute power of the king. The successors of Louis XIV were not able to maintain this position, but the absolute state which was established in France forced recognition of its accomplishments by neighboring states. The latter were driven to admiration and imitation. Thus France pointed the way to the classic form of political organization in the West . . . Even in England an absolute epoch modelled upon the French example took place in the seventeenth century. However, in the long run absolutism was unsuccessful in England.

Under the Stuarts, the doctrine of Divine Right Monarchy was extended so far that the connection between the divine law and the natural law appeared to be weakened, as the possessor of the throne demanded an almost mystical veneration. Parliament successfully defended itself against this overextended concept of sovereignty. In England, it never came to the establishment of a standing army or the formation of a bureaucracy dependent upon the king. Self-government by the English aristocratic class became the insular form of government, but it was only able to establish itself finally after the civil wars. England created for itself a peculiar constitution, according to its own developing political theory, and independent of foreign influence.

During the course of the Reformation, the Anglican church had not changed much in forming its doctrines and practices, except for the abolition of the sacrificial mass. It was likely that it might be brought into a closer relationship with Rome, but Cromwell and his supporters defended themselves against the intention of Charles I. The English monarchy had to yield, because it was opposed by all classes of society, the middle classes of the coastal ports, as well as the Royal Navy, who were all thoroughly Protestant . . . Cromwell's military dictatorship with its standing military commanders exceeded even French absolutism. It was not the death of Cromwell and the restoration of the younger Stuarts but their expulsion by William III of Orange which ended the struggle, and determined that England would not receive an absolute government. But the unified rule which the Parliament embodied after the so-called Glorious Revolution was such a strong opposition to the monarchs that one might even describe it as an insular form of "parliamentary absolutism."

Modern French absolutism was brought to Spain by Louis XIV's grandson Philip V. Here older methods of centralized government had long been in effect, but without destroying local privileges. In Aragon and other provinces the parliamentary bodies of the Cortes had continued to participate in government. These bodies were now no longer summoned to meet (after 1707 in Aragon, 1713 in Castile). Even republics like the [Dutch] States-General and Venice were unable to resist the general trend toward concentration of state power. Russia, at the edge of the European world, sought to adapt to this new development, though it at first did not go beyond a few despotic decrees. In Denmark Fred-

erick III established unlimited monarchy with the Lex Regia (1665). His parliamentary Estates recognized the unrestricted powers of the king by express agreement, so that there came about a unique constitutional establishment of the absolute form of state. The monarchy found allies against the nobility among the clergy and middle class, who greeted absolutism as progress.

In Sweden, which was ruled after 1660 by the nobility represented in the Reichsrat, Charles XI was able to set aside their rule with the support of the peasantry. Thereafter the Estates of Sweden yielded their governmental powers in the 1693 Declaration of Sovereignty. As a result, his successor Charles XII could reign in an extremely absolute manner, neither taking a coronation oath nor receiving ecclesiastical consecration. Not until 1718 did rule by the Estates return. But it was a bizarre absolutism which established itself in Sweden, an unenlightened absolutism which hardened into a militaristic army garrison.

The form of government developed differently in Austria and Prussia. The so-called incontestable rights of Frederick II were philosophically grounded in the social contract. They became transformed into the fulfillment of duty, rather than the personal pleasure of the ruler. The enlightened absolutism in Prussia, which served as a model for the Austrian, rested upon a completely different basis from the contemporary form of government in France which was drawing toward its end.

The governmental type of the absolute monarchy was in itself no new phenomenon, nor was absolutism always and necessarily connected with princely rule, nor were its effects confined to the seventeenth and eighteenth centuries. Absolutism of the period represents a further development of the Renaissance state of western Europe and the princely government of the Reformation age. The essence of the modern state lay in its victory in the conflict between ecclesiastical and secular power, between nobility and monarchy, and in the organization of a centralized administration. Political theory and political practice stood in a close interacting relationship with the practice of government by the absolute princes of the Baroque age. The period saw the composition of political reflections and the gathering of political maxims of important rulers and statesmen, including Richelieu, Louis XIV, the Great Elector, and the Prussian kings Frederick William I and Frederick the Great. These afford us a direct insight into the close connection between theory and practice, of personal and state authority, which were part of absolutism.

In its highest form, the absolute princely state was identified with the person of the monarch. The age strikingly characterized this picture of the prince as the central force of political life in the picture of the *roi soleil,* Louis XIV. The power of the ruler was absolute, that is to say free of obligations and restrictions with regard to the privileges of the parliamentary estates and the traditional state constitution. His rule was sovereign, and the medieval concept of a political hierarchy culminating in the Holy Roman Emperor no longer applied to seventeenth- and eighteenth-century Europe. In addition, the appeal to the divine origin of royal power . . . increased the complete authority of the prince. It is true that the personal utterances of Baroque rulers clearly expressed their attempts to rule in accordance with moral, Christian and just standards. But where the welfare of the state was concerned . . . the princes' decisions were made according to *raison d'état.* The simple formula, the *ragione di stato* of the Italian Renaissance, developed into carefully calculated political action in the age of Cartesian philosophy and the geometrical speculations of Spinoza.

Overall evaluation of the forms of government which are usually grouped together as "absolutism" has changed with increasing distance from the seventeenth century. They are seen in the perspective of much more absolute modern methods of government. The negative image which the older liberalism had of princely absolutism has been modified by our experience with the totalitarian states of the present age. Moreover, since the French Revolution, the idea of the state itself has undergone a transformation, so that it is no longer exactly equivalent to the older concept. The supposedly absolute ruler of the Baroque age was still a long way from the absolutism of the modern democratic state, which had developed in increasing degree since the nineteenth century. . . .

The European absolutism of the seventeenth and eighteenth century was quite other than an amoral despotism given over to power madness and violence. It had strong historical connections with the traditions and privileges of the feudal period, which were often concealed but could not be broken. In an overall view, absolutism appears as a phenomenon of the period which cannot be disregarded, and which was a phase which the modern state had to pass through and master if it was to survive. Everywhere, not only the common subjects, but also the nobility and the royal family were brought into obedience to the state, which was embodied in the person of the king. Even today, one can find traces of this shining conception of princely omnipotence in the fairy tales, with their crowns, ermine robes and carriages, with a life much happier in its way than the turbulent existence of the present.

Absolutism placed all of the citizens in a state of tutelage and stifled a sense of political responsibility. On the other hand it educated them toward an ideal of service and duty, particularly in the later phase of enlightened absolutism, when it was no longer merely a mechanically administered government, and which might perhaps be better described as a late stage of the patriarchal idea of service. . . .

The Nature of Enlightenment

IMMANUEL KANT

As a loyal subject of the enlightened despot Frederick the Great, the Koenigsberg philosopher Immanuel Kant (1724–1804) tried to reconcile the apparently contradictory relationship between freedom and authority which enlightened despotism implied. The following is taken from a little essay entitled "What is Enlightenment?" published in 1784. It offers a thoughtful appraisal of enlightened despotism in practice, and suggests that "a lower degree of civil freedom . . . provides the mind with room for each man to extend himself to his full capacity."

ENLIGHTENMENT is man's release from his self-incurred tutelage. Tutelage is man's inability to make use of his understanding without direction from another. Self-incurred is this tutelage when its cause lies not in lack of reason but in lack of resolution and courage to use it without direction from another. *Sapere aude!* "Have courage to use your own reason!" — that is the motto of enlightenment.

Laziness and cowardice are the reasons why so great a portion of mankind, after nature has long since discharged them from external direction (*naturaliter maiorennes*), nevertheless remains under lifelong tutelage, and why it is so easy for others to set themselves up as their guardians. It is so easy not to be of age. If I have a book which understands for me, a pastor who has a conscience for me, a physician who decides my diet, and so forth, I need not trouble myself. I need not think, if I can only pay — others will readily undertake the irksome work for me.

That the step to competence is held to be very dangerous by the far greater portion of mankind (and by the entire fair sex) — quite apart from its being arduous — is seen to by those guardians who have so kindly assumed superintendence over them. After the guardians have first made their domestic cattle dumb and have made sure that these placid creatures will not dare take a single step without the harness of the cart to which they are tethered, the guardians then show them the danger which threatens if they try to go alone. Actually, however, this danger is not so great, for by falling a few times they would finally learn to walk alone. But an example of this failure makes them timid and ordinarily frightens them away from all further trials.

For any single individual to work himself out of the life under tutelage which has become almost his nature is very difficult. He has come to be fond of this state, and he is for the present really incapable of making use of his reason, for no one has ever let him try it out. Statutes and formulas, those mechanical tools of the rational employment or rather misemployment of his natural gifts, are the fetters of an everlasting tutelage. Whoever throws them off makes only an uncertain leap over the narrowest ditch because he is not accustomed to that kind of free motion. Therefore, there are few who have succeeded by their own exercise of mind both in freeing themselves from incompetence and in achieving a steady pace.

But that the public should enlighten it-

From Immanuel Kant, *On History*, pp. 3–10, translated by Lewis White Beck. Copyright © 1963 by the Liberal Arts Press, Inc., reprinted by permission of the Liberal Arts Press, Inc., a division of the Bobbs-Merrill Company Inc.

self is more possible; indeed, if only freedom is granted, enlightenment is almost sure to follow. For there will always be some independent thinkers, even among the established guardians of the great masses, who, after throwing off the yoke of tutelage from their own shoulders, will disseminate the spirit of the rational appreciation of both their own worth and every man's vocation for thinking for himself. But be it noted that the public, which has first been brought under this yoke by their guardians, forces the guardians themselves to remain bound when it is incited to do so by some of the guardians who are themselves capable of some enlightenment — so harmful is it to implant prejudices, for they later take vengeance on their cultivators or on their descendants. Thus the public can only slowly attain enlightenment. Perhaps a fall of personal despotism or of avaricious or tyrannical oppression may be accomplished by revolution, but never a true reform in ways of thinking. Rather, new prejudices will serve as well as old ones to harness the great unthinking masses.

For this enlightenment, however, nothing is required but freedom, and indeed the most harmless among all the things to which this term can properly be applied. It is the freedom to make public use of one's reason at every point. But I hear on all sides, "Do not argue!" The officer says: "Do not argue but drill!" The tax collector: "Do not argue but pay!" The cleric: "Do not argue but believe!" Only one prince in the world says, "Argue as much as you will, and about what you will, but obey!" Everywhere there is restriction on freedom.

Which restriction is an obstacle to enlightenment, and which is not an obstacle but a promoter of it? I answer: The public use of one's reason must always be free, and it alone can bring about enlightenment among men. The private use of reason, on the other hand, may often be very narrowly restricted without particularly hindering the progress of enlightenment. By the public use of one's reason I understand the use which a person makes of it as a scholar before the reading public. Private use I call that which one may make of it in a particular civil post or office which is entrusted to him. Many affairs which are conducted in the interest of the community require a certain mechanism through which some members of the community must passively conduct themselves with an artificial unanimity, so that the government may direct them to public ends, or at least prevent them from destroying those ends. Here argument is certainly not allowed — one must obey. But so far as a part of the mechanism regards himself at the same time as a member of the whole community or of a society of world citizens, and thus in the role of a scholar who addresses the public (in the proper sense of the word) through his writings, he certainly can argue without hurting the affairs for which he is in part responsible as a passive member. Thus it would be ruinous for an officer in service to debate about the suitability or utility of a command given to him by his superior; he must obey. But the right to make remarks on errors in the military service and to lay them before the public for judgment cannot equitably be refused him as a scholar. The citizen cannot refuse to pay the taxes imposed on him; indeed, an impudent complaint at those levied on him can be punished as a scandal (as it could occasion general refractoriness). But the same person nevertheless does not act contrary to his duty as a citizen when, as a scholar, he publicly expresses his thoughts on the inappropriateness or even the injustice of these levies. Similarly a clergyman is obligated to make his sermon to his pupils in catechism and his congregation conform to the symbol of the church which he serves, for he has been accepted on this condition. But as a scholar he has complete freedom, even the calling, to communicate to the public all his carefully tested and well-meaning thoughts on that which is erroneous in the symbol and to make suggestions for the better organization of the religious body and church. . . .

But would not a society of clergymen,

perhaps a church conference or a venerable classis (as they call themselves among the Dutch), be justified in obligating itself by oath to a certain unchangeable symbol in order to enjoy an unceasing guardianship over each of its members and thereby over the people as a whole, and even to make it eternal? I answer that this is altogether impossible. Such a contract, made to shut off all further enlightenment from the human race, is absolutely null and void even if confirmed by the supreme power, by parliaments, and by the most ceremonious of peace treaties. An age cannot bind itself and ordain to put the succeeding one into such a condition that it cannot extend its (at best very occasional) knowledge, purify itself of errors, and progress in general enlightenment. That would be a crime against human nature, the proper destination of which lies precisely in this progress; and the descendants would be fully justified in rejecting those decrees as having been made in an unwarranted and malicious manner.

The touchstone of everything that can be concluded as a law for a people lies in the question whether the people could have imposed such a law on itself. Now such a religious compact might be possible for a short and definitely limited time, as it were, in expectation of a better. One might let every citizen, and especially the clergyman, in the role of scholar, make his comments freely and publicly, i.e., through writing, on the erroneous aspects of the present institution. The newly introduced order might last until insight into the nature of these things had become so general and widely approved that through uniting their voices (even if not unanimously) they could bring a proposal to the throne to take those congregations under protection which had united into a changed religious organization according to their better ideas, without, however, hindering others who wish to remain in the order. But to unite in a permanent religious institution which is not to be subject to doubt before the public even in the lifetime of one man, and

thereby to make a period of time fruitless in the progress of mankind toward improvement, thus working to the disadvantage of posterity — that is absolutely forbidden. For himself (and only for a short time) a man may postpone enlightenment in what he ought to know, but to renounce it for himself and even more to renounce it for posterity is to injure and trample on the rights of mankind.

And what a people may not decree for itself can even less be decreed for them by a monarch, for his law-giving authority rests on his uniting the general public will in his own. If he only sees to it that all true or alleged improvement stands together with civil order, he can leave it to his subjects to do what they find necessary for their spiritual welfare. This is not his concern, though it is incumbent on him to prevent one of them from violently hindering another in determining and promoting this welfare to the best of his ability. To meddle in these matters lowers his own majesty, since by the writings in which his subjects seek to present their views he may evaluate his own governance. He can do this when, with deepest understanding, he lays upon himself the reproach, "Caesar non est supra grammaticos." Far more does he injure his own majesty when he degrades his supreme power by supporting the ecclesiastical despotism of some tyrants in his state over his other subjects.

If we are asked, "Do we now live in an *enlightened age?*" the answer is, "No," but we do live in an *age of enlightenment*. As things now stand, much is lacking which prevents men from being, or easily becoming, capable of correctly using their own reason in religious matters with assurance and free from outside direction. But, on the other hand, we have clear indications that the field has now been opened wherein men may freely deal with these things and that the obstacles to general enlightenment or the release from self-imposed tutelage are gradually being reduced. In this respect, this is the age of enlightenment, or the century of Frederick.

A prince who does not find it unworthy of himself to say that he holds it to be his duty to prescribe nothing to men in religious matters but to give them complete freedom while renouncing the haughty name of *tolerance,* is himself enlightened and deserves to be esteemed by the grateful world and posterity as the first, at least from the side of government, who divested the human race of its tutelage and left each man free to make use of his reason in matters of conscience. Under him venerable ecclesiastics are allowed, in the role of scholars, and without infringing on their official duties, freely to submit for public testing their judgments and views which here and there diverge from the established symbol. And an even greater freedom is enjoyed by those who are restricted by no official duties. This spirit of freedom spreads beyond this land, even to those in which it must struggle with external obstacles erected by a government which misunderstands its own interest. For an example gives evidence to such a government that in freedom there is not the least cause for concern about public peace and the stability of the community. Men work themselves gradually out of barbarity if only intentional artifices are not made to hold them in it.

I have placed the main point of enlightenment — the escape of men from their self-incurred tutelage — chiefly in matters of religion because our rulers have no interest in playing the guardian with respect to the arts and sciences and also because religious incompetence is not only the most

harmful but also the most degrading of all. But the manner of thinking of the head of a state who favors religious enlightenment goes further, and he sees that there is no danger to his law-giving in allowing his subjects to make public use of their reason and to publish their thoughts on a better formulation of his legislation and even their open-minded criticisms of the laws already made. Of this we have a shining example wherein no monarch is superior to him whom we honor.

But only one who is himself enlightened is not afraid of shadows, and who has a numerous and well-disciplined army to assure public peace, can say: "Argue as much as you will, and about what you will, only obey!" A republic could not dare say such a thing. Here is shown a strange and unexpected trend in human affairs in which almost everything, looked at in the large, is paradoxical. A greater degree of civil freedom appears advantageous to the freedom of mind of the people, and yet it places inescapable limitations upon it; a lower degree of civil freedom, on the contrary, provides the mind with room for each man to extend himself to his full capacity. As nature has uncovered from under this hard shell the seed for which she most tenderly cares — the propensity and vocation to free thinking — this gradually works back upon the character of the people, who thereby gradually become capable of managing freedom; finally, it affects the principles of government, which finds it to its advantage to treat men, who are now more than machines, in accordance with their dignity.

The Philosopher-Prince

VOLTAIRE

Francois-Marie Arouet de Voltaire (1694–1778) the most prominent of the *philosophes* by virtue of his long career and enormous production of plays, poems, histories, political tracts, and novels, was not only a lifetime correspondent of such enlightened despots as Frederick the Great and Catherine the Great, but a firm defender of liberty. In the most recent analysis of his politics, Peter Gay points out that Voltaire was a defender of the *thèse royale*, the idea of royal absolutism, in France. But Gay differs with historians who have ascribed to Voltaire a defense of enlightened despotism, preferring to see him as a defender of a "constitutional absolutism." The following selection is taken from a pamphlet of 1750, "The Voice of the Sage and of the People." It was written to support the efforts of Louis XV to tax the French clergy, but also casts light on Voltaire's ideal of a philosopher-prince, an ideal which he maintained in later life even after his somewhat disillusioning period of residence at the court of Frederick the Great.

Good government consists in protecting and restraining equally all the professions of a state.

Government cannot be good, if it does not have sole power.

In states of mixed form, this power results from the consent of several orders of society, and thus they acquire their unity. Without it, all is confusion.

In any kind of state, the greatest misfortune occurs when the legislative power is opposed. The happiest years of the monarchy were the last years of Henry IV, Louis XIV and Louis XV when the kings governed by themselves.

There should not be two powers in one state.

The distinction between the spiritual and the temporal power is abused. Should I recognize in my own house two masters, myself the father of the family, and the teacher of my children to whom I pay wages? I wish that I would have the greatest respect for the teacher of my children, but I would never wish that he would ever have the least authority in my household.

Disregarding Italy, there are four great states in Europe which are of the Roman communion: France, Spain, the better half of Germany, and Poland. In Spain the government has made an agreement with the Pope to impose taxes on the clergy. The Queen-Empress of Hungary does the same; she received permission in the last war to take the silver from the churches. In Poland the army of the crown is sometimes quartered upon the lands of the clergy because they pay very little towards the republic.

In France, where reason perfects itself daily, that reason teaches us that the Church should contribute to the expenses of the state in proportion to its revenues. The body which has the task of instructing about justice ought to begin by giving an example. . . .

Reason, in perfecting itself, destroys the seed of the wars of religion. The philosophic spirit has banished that pestilence from the world. . . .

Reason teaches us that the prince may allow ancient abuses to continue, like al-

From [Voltaire] *La Voix du Sage et du Peuple* (Amsterdam, 1750), pp. 1–16. Translation by the editor.

lowing certain things to be decided in the court of Rome which could well be decided in his own council.

It shows us that when the prince wishes to abolish such customs they fall like a gothic building which one destroys to rebuild in modern style.

It shows us that when the prince wishes to wipe out an injurious abuse the people ought to support him and will support him, even if it is four thousand years old.

This reason instructs us that the prince ought to be absolute master of all ecclesiastical policy, without any restriction, because ecclesiastical policy is a part of government. Just as the father of the family prescribes for his teacher the hours of instruction, the type of studies etc., so the prince ought to prescribe to all clerics, without exception, whatever has the least connection with the public order.

This reason tells us that when the prince wishes to give to those who have spilt their blood for the state benefices for pensions, that those benefices become part of the patrimony of the state. Not only all the officers of the army, but all the magistrates, all the farmers, all the citizens should praise the prince. Whoever opposes an institution so useful should be regarded as an enemy of his country.

Similarly, when the prince, who is the pastor of his people, wishes to increase his flock as he should, when he wishes to . . . restrain imprudent men and women from taking fatal . . . vows which lead to the extinction of the race, at an age when they are not yet able to manage their own property, society will bless the prince in following centuries.

There are useless monasteries in the world . . . with a revenue of two hundred thousand pounds. Reason proves that if one gave these two hundred thousand pounds to a hundred officers who would be married, there would be one hundred good citizens rewarded, one hundred girls provided for, and within ten years, at least four hundred more persons in the state, in place of fifty do-nothings. Reason shows that these fifty do-nothings given back to the state might cultivate the earth, or people the land, and that there would be more workers and soldiers. This is what everyone desires, from the prince of the blood down to the wine-grower. Only superstition opposes it . . . but reason will erase that superstition. . . .

It is a great fortune for the prince and for the state when there are many philosophers to impress their teachings on the minds of men.

The philosophers have no special interest, and are able to speak only in favor of reason and the public interest.

The philosophers render service to the prince by destroying superstition, which is always the enemy of princes.

It was superstition which assassinated Henry III, Henry IV, William, Prince of Orange, and so many others. It is she which has brought forth rivers of blood since Constantine.

Superstition is the most horrible enemy of the human race. When superstition dominates the prince, it prevents him from doing good for his people; when it dominates the people, it raises them against their prince.

Nowhere on earth is there an example of philosophers who opposed the laws of a prince; there is no single century in which superstition and enthusiasm have not caused troubles which became horrors.

There is not a single example of trouble and dissension when the prince was the absolute master of ecclesiastical policy. There are only examples of disorders and calamities when the clergy were not entirely subject to the prince.

The happiest thing that can happen to men, is for the prince to be a philosopher.

The philosopher-prince acts so that reason, rather than disputes, theological quarrels, enthusiasm and superstition, makes progress in his lands. He furthers the development of reason.

That progress alone will suffice to annihilate in a few years . . . all the disputes about grace, because the number of reasonable men will be increased, the number of eccentric spirits who nourish such absurd opinions will diminish. . . .

The philosopher-prince will encourage that religion which instructs men in a pure and very useful morality. He will put an end to disputes over dogma, because these disputes have never produced anything but evil.

He will administer justice as uniformly as he can, with the least possible delay and blush for our ancestors . . . The philosopher-prince will be convinced that the more a people works, the more it is rich. He will take care that the cities are always being beautified, because this makes for more employment, and the results are both useful and agreeable.

One could compose a great book about all that could be done, but a philosopher-prince would not need a great book.

Theorists of Enlightened Despotism

LEO GERSHOY

Leo Gershoy (1897–   ) a leading American authority on the French Revolution, is the author of several works including *The French Revolution and Napoleon* and *Bertrand Barère, a Reluctant Terrorist*. The following selection is from his *From Despotism to Revolution*, and it discusses the ideas of the French *philosophes* with special reference to the Physiocrats and their concept of *despotisme éclaireé*. Gershoy's account emphasizes the role of the French theorists; other writers like Hartung and Walder, in their selections in this work, lay more stress upon the German and Italian thinkers. Gershoy suggests the importance of the despot as the initiator of reform to the French writers.

VOLTAIRE AND DIDEROT were not un-representative of the older generation of *philosophes,* who in the main helped to gain the advantages of constitutional rule but vaguely expected to attain them by following the road of enlightened monarchical rule. Bourgeois by birth, aristocratic humanist by training and inclination, but *grand seigneur* by social acclimatization, Voltaire was a complete worldling, loving his ease and reveling in the luxury of tasteful adornments. "Every *honnête homme,*" he wrote, "has those views." Confident in man's progress, he was enormously practical and incapable of abandoning a cautious reserve in social matters. He was certainly no radical, not even a democrat. More than once he referred to the masses as *canaille,* certainly without any ill intent but, what is worse, without true consciousness of his prejudice. He had, too, very little specific interest in the details of political theories, and his tireless pen never wrote a systematic treatise on political relations. He was by conviction and temperament an enthusiast of enlightened despotism. His *Age of Louis XIV* can hardly be considered a hostile treatment of the *grand monarque.* His praise of Frederick and his well-rewarded admiration for Catherine were notorious. If he was excited to enthusiasm over the government of China and its civilization, it was because he was convinced that the greatness of that country stemmed from the practical application that the responsible classes of the state made of the teaching of its sages, such as Confucius. If he set great store by the English constitutional arrangement, it was for the benefit of the French middle classes that he courageously extolled the conquests won by their English compeers. With these liberties he remained content in deed and in thought. Even as the deist in him built God a temple, preferring to invent a God even if He did not exist, so the landed proprietor who attacked the cruel absurdities of serfdom shrank from the idea of economic equality. It was a property-conscious liberal who wrote, "We are all equals as men but not equal in society." Manifestly, there was nothing reprehensible in his doing so, but the fact is worth recording. To put the authority of the enlightened prince behind the accomplishment of Voltairian reforms was the real essence of his political credo.

The generous and warmhearted Diderot was torn between two contradictory passions. The moralist and sentimentalist in him propelled him forward to think in egalitarian terms that could be called Rousseauist had they not appeared a full decade before the *Social Contract* saw the light of day. His hatred of privilege and his humanitarian benevolence made him advocate sweeping measures to remedy the existing social inequalities. But there was a Diderot who looked for short cuts to Utopia, who enthusiastically admired Le Mercier's "legal despotism." The Diderot who was the beneficiary of Catherine the Great's largesse drew back from the implications of his sentimental radicalism. In substance he too placed his faith in progress from above. "We will preach against insensate laws until they are reformed," he said, "and meantime we will submit to them." Though he limited the authority of the prince to executing the laws of nature, he made active membership in the state a function of property. "It is property that makes the citizen: every man who has possessions in the state is interested in the state; and . . . it is by reason of his pos-

sessions that he ought to speak, and that he acquires the right of having himself represented. . . ."

Voltaire and Diderot threw out suggestions, but the three volumes of Holbach's *Système sociale ou principes naturelles de la morale et de la politique* (1772–1773) was a true code of enlightened despotism. Rejecting all recourse to supernatural sanctions, Holbach made universal necessity, the complete determinism prevailing in nature and in human nature, the motive force of human conduct. . . .

Morality becomes the necessity of employing the proper means ("fulfilling one's duties") of making happy those with whom we have to live, so that they in turn may make us happy. Were we living in a properly organized society, we would recognize that it is to our own interest to be virtuous, and that self-interest alone is the basis of morality. But experience has shown that the individual is neither always quick enough nor always able to act according to his own interests. Hence he must be aided by more enlightened minds, and "politics ought to be the art of regulating the passions of men, and directing them towards the good of society." By that aphorism Holbach means that the obligations inherent in the natural social pact must be effectively enforced by the sanctions of the law. He is a libertarian for whom true liberty lies in obeying "the laws which remedy the natural inequality of men." Law is equally binding on all members of the state. As the expression of the general will, it ought to restrain the sovereign as well as the people, to define and limit his powers and give the people the right not to obey him when the prince fails "to assure to the greatest number of citizens the advantages for which they are leagued together. These advantages are liberty, property, and security."

Like Rousseau before him, Holbach was manifestly prescribing for the ideal state. His reiterated use of "ought" alone made that clear. The spirit of his thought was democratic; but the letter prescribed enlightened absolutism. While awaiting that happy era when all subjects of the prince would reach the requisite intellectual maturity to share in legislation, the philosopher-king, supported by the intellectual élite, would take a short cut toward Utopia. For all his enticing suggestions, concerning the future, Holbach entrusted man's fate in the present to the prince. Ultimately the prince would become supererogatory, but not until he had dispelled the ignorance that made the people a prey to demagogues and cruel fanatics and achieved his destiny of educating his subjects into the responsibilities of citizenship. . . .

The position of the physiocrats is more difficult of analysis. Experienced and progressive business men and trained, many of them, in government administration, they were also theorists who wove their keen observations about capitalist economics into the pattern of a broad social philosophy. Upon the bases of their utilitarian philosophy of social relations they set a theory of political relations which was symbolized in their own catch phrase of "Legal Despotism." All of them from their revered leader, the court physician Dr. Quesnay, whom they styled the "Confucius of the West," to the humblest of his disciples concerned themselves primarily with economic renovation of France. From firsthand business experience they drew the conclusion that the basic structural flaw was the unjustly conceived and wretchedly administered system of taxation. The first endeavor, accordingly, of these keen capitalist economists was to lay the foundations of a solid fiscal administration. . . .

The fundamental basis of the natural order according to Le Mercier was the right of property. Without it society could have no meaning. All governmental activity should "trend toward the greatest possible increase of production and population and assure the greatest possible happiness to those living in society." But less pontifically, it was the duty of the state, through the person of the "legal despot," to guarantee the rights of property, security, and that

free competition which they deemed the mainspring of human perfectibility. The most vital link between the "legal despot" and his subjects being the system of taxation, "therefore," argued Le Mercier, "by reason of the fact that this public revenue for annual expenditures can be maintained only by annual replenishing, it is evident that this public revenue can be nothing else but a portion of the value of production which the soil gives every year." Here was the great panacea for the fiscal ills of society, and for the evils that swept in the train of inequitable taxation: the single tax upon the land, their famous *impôt unique*. However, this single tax could not be equitably assessed until the monarchy had first set up a *cadastre*, or public registration, giving a catalogued statement of the location, extent, and value of the landed property in the realm. Once instituted, the single tax brought it within the realm of possibility to rationalize the whole of agricultural life. The augmented revenues of the state would be more than ample to finance the necessary economic improvements: abolition of the vexatious survivals of feudalism in the hunting and fishing rights, the grant of advances and subsidies to progressive proprietors, the improvement of means of transportation, and introduction of the absolute freedom of grain trade throughout the length and breadth of the kingdom.

Fiscal reforms and the increase of agricultural production would be incomplete without a similar guarantee of individual rights in other fields of economic endeavor. To assure the individual his full rights to possess property, to work, buy, and sell in perfect freedom, it was also necessary to abolish corporate guilds and introduce a free internal transit in human and intellectual resources as well as in goods and money. Money, men, and materials had to be brought together when and where they were most needed with the minimum of regulation and red tape. Their "natural and essential order" connoted peace in international relations as well as tranquillity within each country. It implied a federation of nations, a kind of holy alliance of proprietors, bound to one another by self-interest to end the scourge of ruinous war and, through free trade for all, gain security for each. Finally, all this program of material advance would remain otiose unless the citizen were concurrently protected in his less material interests, in his right to speak and write freely and believe as his conscience impelled him to believe; above all, his right to receive that public instruction which would some day make him too like unto a king. . . .

By their stress upon man's liberties, and his capacity along with his right to be responsible for his destiny, the physiocrats seemed to take an unequivocal stand with the champions of individualism. They appeared thus at the antipodes of the cameralists who would attain order through "the dextrous manipulations of a skillful politician." Nevertheless, this stand was more apparent than real. The heart of their political doctrine was the way in which the legal despot fulfilled what Le Mercier called "the obligations laid upon sovereigns to promulgate by positive ordinances the natural and essential laws of the social order." Again and again they made clear that state activity had to continue and that these liberties could not be secured save by the singleness of political authority. "It is the essence of authority," intoned Le Mercier, "that to separate it and divide it, is to render it incapable of action and in consequence to nullify it."

Their legal despotism was in fact a gigantic effort at compromise between monarchical and individual rights. In a way it was also a threat that amounted to saying to rulers that this was how monarchs should govern, if their propertied subjects would allow them to govern at all. Each contemporary prince, sitting on his throne, could satisfy their requirements, provided that he, "the single force and single unity," agreed to chart his policy under the guidance of the laws which their wisdom had discovered. Their doctrine thus transformed the absolute prince into the "legal despot. . . ." For the moment he was to accept the counsel of a quasi-senate of landed proprietors. When, however, in the fullness of philosophical time, all his subjects were sufficiently educated, he would have to rely upon a broader enlightened public opinion.

All that these warmhearted reformers, these foes of clerical asceticism and enemies of aristocratic and monarchical absurdities, could do was to bring themselves to a sort of negative, restricted individualism. The absolute monarch was their foe, the enemy of the upper middle classes whom they represented, but they would not have the propertyless as their associates in the struggle for power. The ruler they would tame, bloodlessly, without violence, binding him by the restraints of the law. To the masses, whom their doctrine also endowed with rights, they counseled patience. They were agreed to unravel the web of governmental regulations, but slowly and with discretion. They left much for the state to perform in maintaining law and order, in public administration, in education and social welfare. They permitted themselves the exercise of their natural right to negotiate as equals with the monarch, but they hesitated to place the burden of such heavy responsibilities upon the untutored and the unpropertied. . . .

These champions of enlightened despotism dwelt in a strange political no-man's-land, a border country still reminiscent of the familiar topography of old regime absolutism, but verging upon the new terrain of parliamentary constitutionalism. When rulers stood on the defensive, calling themselves the first servants of the state, writing political "testaments" for the edification of their successors, and doing vicarious penance through their own heightened welfare activities for their predecessors' sins of omission, the intellectual élite also grasped at the opportunity to make princes useful to society. The more conservative frankly defended monarchical institutions on historical grounds, adapting and extending state activity to newer needs. The more liberal of the liberal-conservatives narrowed the range of state action without daring to eliminate it entirely. Resigning their children and grandchildren to the seemly tranquillity of a world without princes, they made the best of the present world by keeping the prince on his throne, but in leading strings of purple. . . .

The Philosophers and the Kings

PAUL HAZARD

One of the most brilliant French writers on the history of modern thought, Paul Hazard (1878–1944) described the evolution of European ideas from the seventeenth century to the romantic period. The following selection from his history of European thought in the eighteenth century demonstrates the shortcomings of enlightened despotism when viewed by an historian warmly sympathetic to the liberal ideas of the enlightenment. Hazard poses the question: what was the real relationship between the philosophers and the kings?

You MIGHT HAVE thought you were looking at a minuet: the Princes bow to the Philosophers, the Philosophers return the bow. As if the mighty ones had forgotten how they had persecuted, and were still persecuting, writers who were trying to undermine their authority; and as if the writers had forgotten about the furious rhetoric they had hurled, and were still hurling, against the tyrants! They declared that for ages past all that kings had done was to strive to put chains about their people, and they bowed low to those same kings! Despotism was getting to mean something new. All that had to be done was to tack on an adjective and call it "enlightened" despotism.

Certainly, the phenomenon was not a little complex; you could, if you tried, find some points of contact between this enlightened despotism and the philosophy of light, which would go some way towards explaining the misapprehension. The enlightened despots were warring against privilege, and that, to begin with, was a common line of action. They contemplated a vast egalitarian reform, they were for destroying all traces, and there were still too many, of the old feudal system. Ardently progressive, they adopted any economic measure that might be calculated to advance the prosperity of their respective peoples. The philosophers were useful because they gave lustre to their reign. And then, most important of all, the centralized administration which they set going, created order in place of disorder; order the mirrored image of universal reason; they were rationalizing government. Reason, no sooner invoked, promptly supported their policy: Euclid, too, was a despot. One might go so far as to say that it belonged to the mind that was the strongest, the intelligence that was the most clear-sighted, and to the understanding that was the most unerring, to be a ruler; so that inherited power was sanctioned in their case by natural law. More than that; if utility was the sole measure of right behaviour, why should not a great nation subjugate one in which the standard of life was lower? Why should it be taxed with wrongdoing, if the

From Paul Hazard, *European Thought in the Eighteenth Century* (New Haven, 1954), pp. 328–334. Reprinted by permission of Librairie A. Hatier and Yale University Press.

result of its conquests was a further substantial addition to the sum-total of human happiness?

But whatever might seem to be the possibilities of agreement, they did but mask a basic, an irreconcilable antagonism: on the one side, the totalitarian State directing and controlling all the activities of its members; on the other side, the liberal or constitutional State. If those who argued in favour of the liberal form of government made common cause with the representatives of despotism, they were betraying their own political philosophy. You either had to bend nature to your will, or else let her have a free hand; either the maximum of interference, or the minimum. Either the spontaneous virtue of the eternal laws, or the will of one man dominating everything, the law included.

A form of government was coming to the fore in Europe which took no stock of constitutions, the balance of power, and the uneasy suspicion that some one power might outstrip all the others. The die had been cast in 1740, when Frederick II succeeded the Roi-Sergent. Farewell to anti-Machiavellianism! What he had to do now was to get to know his business; curb his impulsiveness; overcome his horror of the battlefield, his fear; find out people's weak spots the better to profit by them; get command of his physique and, when his mind said "march," make his body obey; make the most of his unrivalled intelligence; become the cleverest of the clever, the strongest of the strong; foreign policy, war, civil administration, finance, industry and even education — all these he must take in hand. Everything, down to the smallest detail, must depend upon one sole central will. He must transform his present meagre inheritance into one of the first, and if possible, *the* first, power in Europe. That was his task. He was not merely the servant of the State; he *was* the State. Never, throughout that century, was there a more arresting personality, and the age contemplated him with admiration. Between the poet, the musician, the dilettante of Rheinsberg and Old Fritz with his dirty clothes,

his limbs deformed by gout, his nose all stained with snuff, how many different beings were united in one? The general who on the night of battle recites Racine, and imagines himself one of Racine's heroes. The traveller summoning to his carriage-door burgomasters and justices; who questions the peasants about their ploughlands, about their cows, and the supply of salt. The ironist, the high-and-mighty one, the "quiz," the jester, the skin-flint who counted every farthing, and the man of genius. The tireless official who has his subordinates up before him in his office and wants almost as much out of them as he takes out of himself. Then there is the philosopher of Sans-Souci, and the artful diplomatist, who checkmates Austria, France, and England, though his procedure may be a little questionable, though he may hit below the belt. And besides these, a host of other incarnations, all of them, by divers routes, making for one and the same goal: the greatness of Prussia.

Over against him, face to face, behold his adversary, Maria Theresa; and when her time comes to pass on into the chapel of the Capuchins, to take her place in the vault of the Hapsburgs, behold her son, Joseph II! A despot doing his best to play the kindly father of his people, looking on his imperial office as a sacred mission, trying, and trying in vain, to make everybody happy. Unification, centralization, rationalization, these were the aims that he pursued, hurrying from Vienna to Budapest, to Prague, to Brussels, to see everything for himself, give an eye to everything, and suffer nothing to remain as it was, never doubting the fundamental wisdom of his decrees, decrees which had merely to be promulgated in order to become immediately effective; turning everything upside down, in his zeal for improvement. There was something touching about this zeal of his, this passion for the public good. Headstrong, irritable, impetuous; sick with fatigue and exhaustion, working himself to death, heart-broken to see that men refused to be angels or to recognize as a beneficent archangel this Emperor of theirs who wore the twin aureole of Enlightenment and Right Divine. Yet he had done his utmost to bring everything, the Church included, under state-control. In 1763, while he was still getting his hand in, so to speak, there appeared a book which created a wide sensation: *Justini Febronii J.C. de statu Ecclesiae et legitima potestate Romani Pontificis liber singularis.* Under the name Febronius was concealed, with a care and a success that few incognitos have achieved, the name of the author, who was none other than Hontheim, Bishop-suffragan of Treves. The thesis he put forward was well calculated to produce a shock throughout the length and breadth of Christendom. It amounted to saying that the Papal rule had been but one long usurpation; that the time had arrived to replace it by an oligarchy of bishops, a body itself deriving its authority by delation from the democracy of the priests and the faithful. The Pope was to be left in possession of his executive functions, but the legislative power was to reside with him no longer; the power to define doctrines binding on the Church Universal was to belong exclusively to the General Councils. To bring about this reform, it would be necessary for the Pope himself to play his part, as well as the prelacy, the theologians and the monarch. The latter was to sustain the preponderating rôle. He was sovereign Lord over his subjects, and he would protect them against all papal and ecclesiastical encroachment. . . . All this was a compound of Jansenism and natural law, reinforced by all the arguments against Rome that had ever been made to do duty. To those monarchs whose policy it was that religion should not be a power apart, but a department subject to their royal jurisdiction, the occasion was far too tempting a one to be neglected; but Febronius's best disciple was Joseph II.

Catherine II suffered nature to have her way, in so far as her private life was concerned, and her favourites knew well enough how imperious were nature's demands upon her. But it was to the service of the Russian State, to the welfare and advancement of Russia that she devoted her sovereign intellectual gifts, her political sagacity, and all the power of her will. She allowed herself no rest till two objects had been attained: in the foreign sphere, the destruction of Poland, the weakening of Turkey and the dismemberment of Sweden; in the domestic sphere, the establishment of her authority in place of the anarchy in which her immediate predecessors had left the Empire; Catherine the Great would resume the task of Peter the Great. A woman of genius, the Comte de Ségur called her. "Proud, tenderhearted and victorious," like Louis XIV, said the Prince de Ligne.

There were other monarchs who were included in the category of enlightened despots, Gustavus III of Sweden, Christian VII of Denmark, Stanislas Augustus of Poland, and even Charles III of Spain; and when sovereigns ran short, there were the ministers who supported them; there was Charles III's Count d'Aranda; Pombal was Joseph I's right-hand man; there was Dutillot at Parma, Tanucci at Naples. All were striking, powerful personalities, very different from those lily-faced sons of Telemachus whom the philosophers depicted as representing the ideal of kingship. To this imperious breed, to these realists who acknowledged no reason but reasons of State, to these spiritual sons of Machiavelli, the apostles of the English constitution addressed their smiles of approval. Not perhaps quite so freely in the case of Joseph II; but without any reservation whatever in that of Pombal, since he had expelled the Jesuits; for that is what it always came back to. "Down with the Church!" was always the rallying cry. They also fully approved of d'Aranda, Dutillot, and Tanucci; and when they came to Catherine II, their encomiums knew no bounds, and they indulged in more flowers of rhetoric than the most abject of sycophants. She was the Semiramis of the North; Algarotti discovered Paradise itself amid the snows of Russia; Carlo Gastone della Torre di Rezzonico dedicated his *Ra-*

gionamento sulla filosofia del secolo XVIII (1778) to Her Imperial Majesty; a pact signed and sealed between Philosophy and the State. She had announced her intention of bestowing a Code on her subjects, and to this end she summoned to a conference in Moscow, deputies from all her provinces, and told them that the country was not made for the sovereign, but the sovereign for the country. She had ideas for reforming the whole legal system, for bringing educational methods up to date. She invited artists to adorn her palaces and her capital; she wanted to have an *Encyclopédiste* as her grandson's tutor, and, in default of d'Alembert, she engaged a Swiss republican; she kept up a friendly correspondence with Mme Geoffrin. When Robertson published his *History of Charles V*, she sent him a gold snuff-box and gave him to understand that his book went with her on all her travels; either that, or Montesquieu's *Esprit des Lois*; and she had Marmontel's *Bélisaire* translated into Russian. As for Diderot, her protégé, her client, who said the only journey he ever wanted to make was to St. Petersburg, you ought to have heard him giving vent to his enthusiasm! If she had a fault, it was that she was too kind; there was not a trace of the despot in her character, in her purposes, or in her deeds. You felt you were a slave in the countries that called themselves free, but over there, in *her* country, you breathed the very air of freedom. But the man the philosophers loved most of all was the representative of the Leviathan State, Frederick II. He, they said, was greater than the greatest of the Roman emperors. He had bestowed happiness on his people, provided Europe with the pattern of the model ruler, and paved the way for the happiness of generations to come. And so on, and so on. Because he was himself a philosopher and had taken the trouble to study the systems that purported to reveal the meaning of life; because he had a very real love of letters and was, in a sense, a man of letters himself; because he gave asylum in his

Academy to all who suffered persecution in the cause of freedom of thought; because he was a deist, and, in his inmost heart, something more than that, in short an atheist; and because he was a genius — for all these reasons, "the philosophers and men of letters in every land have long looked upon you, Sire, as their leader and their model."

We all know how these princes and their successors behaved later on, when the French Revolution translated these philosophers' ideas into action; we all know about the Holy Alliance. But even now, in private, when, that is to say, they were not addressing the sovereigns themselves, the panegyrists felt obliged to voice some doubts as to the manner in which their allies were giving effect to natural law. They did not find it at all convenient to justify the invasion of Silesia; just as the woman who was changed into a cat began chasing mice, so the monarch, as soon as he sees a province he would like, discards his philosopher's mantle and grasps his sword. Solomon, when looked into, brought about a certain amount of disillusionment; his language needed special dictionary interpretation: "My friend" meant "My slave"; "My dear friend" meant "You are not completely indifferent to me." By "I will make you happy," understand "I will put up with you as long as I have need of you." A rumour got about that Catherine II had had her husband murdered, in order that she might rule; an unpleasant story, which it would be well to hush up; people like that were hardly pupils to be proud of. Ah well; one must love one's friends, such as they were; even if they undertook wars of aggression; even though they bled their subjects white in order to keep adding to their standing armies; even if they were false to their sworn oath; even if they partitioned Poland. That was the error; the philosophers thought they were using the kings, and it was the kings who were using them.

A Definition of Enlightened Despotism

FRITZ HARTUNG

Fritz Hartung (1883–   ) is the leading German constitutional historian
and a professor emeritus of the University of Berlin. A long-time student of
the development of European absolutism, Hartung took part in the discussions
of enlightened despotism initiated by the International Historical Congress of
1928. His developing views on the nature of absolutism can be traced in a
variety of publications, including the revisions of his *Deutsche Verfassungsge-
schichte*. In this selection Hartung draws upon work done in collaboration
with Roland Mousnier on a report concerning absolutism for the 1955 Rome
Historical Congress. By way of summing up a generation of work on enlightened despotism, Hartung appeals for greater limitation and precision in
terminology. He prefers to use the expression "enlightened absolutism" and
to restrict its application to Europe in the pre-1789 period.

I WOULD PREFER the expression "enlightened absolutism." I think that it
would be more appropriate to use this term,
because it conforms to the older European
practice of distinguishing clearly between
absolutism — a form of government unrestricted by class or parliamentary institutions, but voluntarily bound by laws and
the rights of the subject — and despotism,
with its unlimited tyranny. If we want to
get a clear idea of the nature of enlightened absolutism, we should not deviate
from the accepted meaning of the word
absolutism. This is, as we have indicated,
a monarchical government which is unrestricted in the use of its powers by the cooperation or approval of a parliamentary
assembly or other autonomous body. It is
not useful to include in the definition
oligarchies or limited aristocracies, still less
democratic tyrannies, whether dictatorial
or caesaristic in form.

If we clearly agree that monarchical absolutism is an essential part of the concept,
then the adjective "enlightened" requires
more exact definition. The work of the
[International Historical] Commission has
shown that we wander too far afield when
we try to include under "enlightened absolutism" every reform attempted by the
power of an absolute monarch. Efforts to
increase the powers of the state by improving the administration and army, by increasing income by a purposeful cultivation
of the economy along mercantilistic lines,
cannot be taken as marks of enlightened
absolutism unless one is ready to concede
that not only Frederick William I of Prussia, but also . . . Peter the Great were enlightened monarchs, or unless one holds
with Lefebvre that the whole development
of absolutism from the fifteenth century
was "an outline sketch of enlightened despotism." We will be able to arrive at a
workable definition if we use the term "enlightened" in the usual sense of what historians understand as "the Enlightenment."
I would characterize enlightened absolutism as a form of government strongly influenced by philosophy, especially the
political philosophy of the enlightenment.
But it should also be noted that an investigation of theory alone will not suffice. . . .

The enlightened ideas of Catherine the

From Fritz Hartung, "Der aufgeklärte Absolutismus," *Historische Zeitschrift*, CLXXX (1955), pp.
19–25. Reprinted by permission of Fritz Hartung and R. Oldenbourg Verlag. Translation by the
editor.

Great had only small influence upon her practice of government, especially in the later years of her reign. The book on the foundations of enlightened absolutism which P. Klassen published in 1929 independently of the work of the International Committee shows how inadequate a one-sided consideration of theory alone can be. This is so because the most beautifully thought-out ideas of scholars have rarely changed the world. It was the essential contribution of enlightened absolutism that it did not remain at theoretical conceptions, but made the attempt to improve existing reality on the basis of its new understanding. Political practice forms a basic part of its essential ideas.

By placing enlightened absolutism in close connection with the eighteenth-century enlightenment, we can not only gain a clear delimitation of its intellectual content, but also place it clearly in its chronological context, a necessary part of historical investigation. We can thus derive a clear conception of the social and economic basis of this historical phenomenon.

Enlightened absolutism was the final phase in the history of the hierarchical feudal society which descended from the middle ages. Already, it had begun to doubt the rightness of the inherited division of society into classes determined by birth, and in having a privileged nobility which stood in contrast to a less-free middle class and an unfree peasantry. It strove to alleviate the inadequacies and hardships of the system, but it lacked the courage to draw the full consequences of its ideas, and to overthrow the whole existing social order.

This article will deal in these pages only with the conditions of this specific period. As far as theory is concerned, it cannot be denied that the special doctrine of *despotisme éclairé* developed in the 1760's was a political off-shoot of the economic doctrines of the Physiocrats. The basic idea of the Physiocrats was expressed in their name. They considered the economic and social order which they found in contemporary France, with its mercantilist economic policy which favored industry at the expense of agriculture, to be a violation of the natural order. This natural order was founded upon the freedom of the individual, especially in economic matters, with liberty to choose an occupation, to engage in business as one saw fit, to have the freedom and security of owning property. Any interference with the natural development of economic life by state intervention was thoroughly rejected, for it was not only an infringement on the natural rights of the individual . . . but also economically harmful. One of the lesser-known Physiocrats, Gournay, summed up the program of the school as: *Laisser faire, laisser passer.* Quesnay, founder of the school and personal physician to Louis XV was supposed to have been asked by Louis, "what would he do if he were king?" "Nothing," he replied. "Who then would rule?" questioned the king, and he was supposed to have answered, "the laws."

Such an attitude presupposed that the natural order of the Physiocrats was already in existence. But since this order had been destroyed for centuries, the state could not be content with the policy of *laisser faire*. On the contrary, it was necessary to use despotic power to restore the natural order, to remove the barriers to the free development of productive forces, and to overcome the resistance of those who were interested in preserving the old order. This [exercise of power] was not to be arbitrary but legal. The law by which it was to guide itself was the law of logic, of logical evidence, the agreement between enlightened thought and planned practical measures. This law of logic would have the same force upon the political field as the laws of Euclid in mathematics. The task of the enlightened despot would be "to recognize, to proclaim and to make respected the natural law, and to restore the natural order." In order to carry out this duty, the monarch must possess the undisputed powers of the state. The Physiocrats had such trust in the victorious power

of the Enlightenment that they advocated
hereditary monarchy without any limitations and energetically rejected any restrictions upon the royal powers, either by the
division of powers which Montesquieu suggested, or by parliamentary control. But
they did demand the right of free intellectual discussion. . . .

Alongside this French doctrine, which
expressly recognized an enlightened despotism, the German political thought of
the eighteenth century deserves consideration in a history of enlightened absolutism.
Though the term is not used, German
thought rested upon the same basis. Unlike the Physiocrats, the German writers
did not make such comprehensive demands
upon the developing state; they had their
origin in the school of Cameralism which
had developed since the sixteenth and seventeenth centuries along with the German
territorial states, and which emerged as a
distinctive contribution to the eighteenth-
century enlightenment.

Christian Wolff was the first to introduce
the ideas of the enlightenment into German administrative theory, which had
been based previously upon biblical precepts and practical experience. His *Rational Considerations on the Social Life of
Mankind,* published in 1721, contains the
chief points of the program which became
characteristic for enlightened absolutism
in Germany. It was based on the enlightenment, to the extent that it began with
the individual, who was recognized as pos-
sessing special "human rights." The state
was ascribed to a free social contract between the people, and its goal was "the
furthering of the common good and security." But it was also absolutistic, since the
individual was given no possibility of forc-
ing the state to respect his rights. On the
contrary: because the state had the duty to
plan and carry out measures for the "furthering of the common welfare and security" it had the right to force citizens to
obey its decrees. The subject was expressly
bound to do willingly whatever the authorities decided was right. Wolff drew up a

detailed program for the practical application of these principles. . . . Dilthey described it appropriately as "the greatest extension of the powers of the state since
Plato." Its basis was derived from the obligation of the state to realize the common
good.

German political theorists of the eighteenth century, especially the disciples of
Wolff, developed these ideas of the police
or welfare powers of the state without con-
tributing anything essentially new. They
liberated administrative doctrine from the
narrow concentration on the financial interest of the prince which had characterized
the older Cameralism. The leading theorists of the movement, Justi, Sonnenfels,
and Martini showed an increasing tendency towards reform under the influence
of the enlightenment, but remained convinced that mankind had not yet come of
age and that it must be forced to accept
what was good for it. This tendency
reached its peak late in the century as it
attempted to supervise the citizen from the
cradle to the grave, and even into the grave,
with government orders and regulations.
The Halle professor G. F. Lamprecht in
his *Attempt at a Complete System of Political Theory* (1784) . . . gave the state
the duty of making the citizens "in every
way better behaved, healthier, wiser,
wealthier, and more secure." It was to provide for them "the comforts and pleasures of
life." How far his humane program of reg-
imentation led him may be demonstrated
by a few of his suggestions. He recommended that all cities should if possible be
the same size, that all streets cross at right
angles, that the coloring of easter eggs was
to be prohibited, and that mothers be
forced to nurse their children." The highest goal was declared to be the welfare of
his subject and the "furthering of his happiness."

. . . The practice of enlightened absolutism was certainly not so radical. The
Physiocrats never progressed beyond the
first stages of implementing their theories.
Though one of their representatives, Tur-

got, became Controller-General of Finances and director of French economic policy, he was not able to put through any substantial amount of his reform program in the face of opposition from the privileged classes (which included in this instance also the wealthy upper middle class!). To his own sorrow, and that of his country, Louis XVI was anything but an enlightened despot. . . .

More important were the contacts which Catherine the Great made with the French enlightened thinkers, including advocates of the theory of *despotisme éclairé*. But they had almost no practical effect upon her conduct of government. In certain particulars, such as the founding of an economic society in 1765, a Physiocratic influence can be detected. But the famous *Instruction* for the assembly of deputies of 1767, which was essentially composed by Catherine herself, was in no way expressive of the theories of *despotisme éclairé*, but was based for the most part upon Montesquieu. Although it rejected the limited

monarchy as unsuited for Russian conditions, its ideas derive from the general enlightenment, not specifically from the Physiocrats. The same holds true for the reforms which the empress carried out in the area of administration. Thus the French doctrine of *despotisme éclairé* was an interesting play of ideas, but remained insignificant in its practical effects. . . .

Nor would I evaluate too highly the direct influence of the above mentioned German administrative theories of the eighteenth century. . . . The theoretical basis of enlightened absolutism, as it appeared in the states of Europe in the second half of the eighteenth century, was . . . derived from the broad background of the thought of the Enlightenment. This is all that it is necessary to say. As Pirenne pointed out, enlightened absolutism was really nothing new, but rather a new version of the old idea of the prince as father of his country, with the difference that what had hitherto sprung from the heart was now to be determined by reason. . . .

II. THREE ENLIGHTENED DESPOTS:
FREDERICK II, JOSEPH II, CATHERINE II

Frederick the *Philosophe*

G. P. GOOCH

George Peabody Gooch (1873–   ), a prolific historian with a wide range of scholarly interests in European history, is the author of many works including *Germany and the French Revolution, Frederick the Great, Catherine the Great,* and *Maria Theresa.* An honorary Fellow of Trinity College, Cambridge, Gooch is thoroughly familiar with the writings and letters of the major enlightened despots. His description of Frederick not only sketches the Prussian king's character but also portrays Frederick's interest in the enlightenment as seen in his own political writings.

O F THE THREE leading Enlightened Autocrats of the eighteenth century Frederick the Great is the earliest and the most eminent. Here, if anywhere, was to be found Plato's Philosopher King, equally interested in power politics and in the things of the mind. Unlike the makers of Prussia — the Great Elector, Frederick I and Frederick William I — Old Fritz was the first and only Hohenzollern *Philosophe,* historian, political thinker, poet, musician. No ruler of modern times has approached him in the range of his interests and the importance of his writings.

While the Crown Prince Frederick William was waiting for the throne his father drew up a Political Testament coloured by the religious feeling of the era of North German Pietism. "Since my twentieth year I have put my whole trust in God, and continually besought Him to hear me, and He has heard my prayer." Rulers who kept God before their eyes and did not keep mistresses would receive abundant bless-ings. Plays and operas, ballets and fancy balls, gluttony and drunkenness are frowned upon by the royal Puritan who preached and practised the strenuous life. Dealing first with the army, he threatens his son with the loss of his blessing if he reduces its strength or neglects its discipline. "You alone must control the revenue and keep the command of the army firmly in your hands. Officers and officials must know that you hold the purse strings." Even more important was the example of the monarch himself. "You must work as I have done. A ruler must attend to all his affairs, for rulers are ordained for work, not for idle, effeminate lives such as, alas, are led by most great people." In the economic sphere the author, like his contemporaries, is a mercantilist. Population is wealth. Towns must be founded, textiles and other industries established. "A country without industries is a body without life, always poor and wretched." Mindful of the debts left by his extravagant father,

From G. P. Gooch, "Der aufgeklärte Absolutismus," *Historia Mundi,* vol. IX, *Aufklärung und Revolution* (Bonn, 1960), pp. 62–74. Reprinted by permission of Verlag A. Francke and G. P. Gooch, who kindly made his original English draft available to the editor for this volume.

Frederick William I urges his son to save a fixed annual sum instead of raising new loans. He should travel through every province once a year to see that everything is in order. Churches and schools should be built. Lutherans and Calvinists should not be allowed to quarrel; Catholics, except the Jesuits, should be tolerated; foreign Jews should not be allowed to enter the kingdom. The passages of this Political Testament on the army, strict economy, religious toleration and annual visits to every corner of his dominions might have been written by his greater son.

The earliest political declaration of Frederick the Great, the so-called Natzmer Letter, written at the age of nineteen, argues that Prussia's scattered territories demand consolidation. "In due time the King of Prussia could play a fine part among the great ones of the earth, giving or preserving peace only from love of justice, not from fear, and, if the honour of the dynasty and the country demand war, being able to wage it with vigour, fearing no enemy except the anger of heaven, which need not be apprehended while piety and the love of justice prevail over irreligion and faction, avarice and interest. I hope that this House of Prussia will raise itself high above the dust in which it has lain, so that it may cause the Protestant religion to flourish in Europe and the Empire, that it may be the resource of the afflicted, the support of widows and orphans, the friend of the poor, the enemy of the unjust. If it were changed, if injustice, religious indifference, partiality or vice should prevail over virtue, which God forbid, I wish its fall to be quicker than its rise."

Seven years later the Crown Prince wrote his *Considérations sur l'état présent du corps politique de l'Europe.* Men, he declares, are the same in all times and countries, similar passions and inclinations leading to similar results. Princes share two common failings—ambition and laziness. "The policy of great monarchies has never varied. Their fundamental principle has been ceaseless aggrandizement; their

wisdom has consisted in anticipating the wiles of their enemies and in winning the contest of wits. Many princes believe that their subjects are created for their grandeur and their pride, mere instruments of their unruly passions. Hence the cult of false glory, the instinct of aggression, the severity of taxation, the idleness, pride, injustice, inhumanity, tyranny of the ruler. If he would trace the authority of his house back to its source he would learn that the elevation of its first member was the work of the people, and that the thousands committed to his charge did not enslave themselves to an individual in order to increase his power or to become the victims of his caprice. They chose the man whom they thought the most just, the most fatherly, the most humane, the most capable of defending them against their enemies, the most prudent in avoiding ruinous wars." Here is the doctrine of the Social Contract, though in none of his political treatises does he draw the logical conclusion that if the ruler breaks the contract and becomes the scourge of his people they have a right to resist. Like James I and Louis XIV, Bossuet and the Cameralists, the moral obligation of the ruler to do his duty is fully recognised, but no penalty can be imposed if he sins. The doctrine of accountability, which the execution of Charles I and the expulsion of James II had established in England, found little favour with Continental publicists till the second half of the eighteenth century. To avoid the necessity either of authorising or forbidding resistance to misgovernment, Montesquieu recommended a division of power on the English model as most likely to avoid political strife.

L'Antimachiavel, the third and last of Frederick's political treatises before his accession, denounces *The Prince* as one of the most dangerous books ever written, the product of a semi-barbarous age. Since rulers were instituted for the protection and well-being of the community, the sovereign, far from being the absolute master, is merely *le premier domestique du peuple.*

Like Montesquieu he avoids the problem of the right of resistance if the ruler breaks his contract. Inheriting the Prussian tradition of absolutism, he neither demands passive obedience in all circumstances, like Hobbes and Bossuet, nor explicitly permits resistance, but tacitly assumes that the ruler knows best and that his subjects will obey. How indeed could public opinion express itself effectively in the absence of representative institutions and a free press? "A contented people will not think of revolt, for its prince is its benefactor, and the sovereign fears no diminution of his power. The Dutch would never have risen against the Spaniards if their tyranny had not been so flagrant." That there may be limits to human endurance is thus implicitly recognised without affecting the fabric of his thought. Limited monarchy might suit the English, but no one dreamed of it in Germany which Herder called the land of obedience.

To Machiavelli's argument that virtue in a wicked world leads to catastrophe Frederick rejoins that to avoid disaster we must be good as well as prudent. A good King is well served. Discipline is needed for the army, but "on the day of battle I would rather be loved than feared by my soldiers. The King of England knows that he has nothing to fear unless he himself provokes a storm. A cruel prince is likely to be betrayed, for cruelty is insupportable. In the management of foreign affairs — the most difficult task of a ruler — the prince cannot always avoid the regrettable necessity of breaking a treaty or an alliance when compelled to act for the safety of the state, which may also justify recourse to war. Wars are of three kinds — defence, interest and prevention." . . . All wars are just which resist usurpers, maintain legitimate rights, safeguard the liberty of the world, and oppose the violence of ambitious men. The sovereigns who wage such wars need not reproach themselves with the shedding of blood. In their dealings with foreign states the Enlightened Autocrats were no better Europeans than their prede-

cessors or successors. In this celebrated political treatise we find the three main pillars of *Realpolitik* — the frank acceptance of *Staatsräson,* the Balance of Power, and the permission of offensive war. Since the authors of *The Prince* and *l'Antimachiavel* agree that a ruler can do whatever he thinks fit the Prussian prince had no right to throw stones at the Florentine publicist.

Frederick's Political Testaments of 1752 and 1768 embody the ripe experience of an experienced ruler. Government, he begins, is concerned with four main problems — justice, finance, the army, policy. In the first of these departments judges of the highest character must be chosen and the ruler should never interfere with their work. But he must always watch their conduct and punish them if they fail in their duty. In finance, on the other hand, the ruler must himself take the lead. If a country is to be happy and a prince is to be respected, he must keep his house in order. The revenue should be increased, not by imposing new taxes, but by improving the soil and fostering industry; and part of the annual yield should be kept as a reserve in case of war or any other calamity. The privileges and therefore the prestige of the nobility must be preserved since their record of service was good. In ecclesiastical matters tolerance must be the rule, not only because "all religions, when one looks into them, are seen to rest on fables," but for the sake of peace. Everyone could find his own way to heaven. "I am in a way the Pope of the Lutherans and the head of the Reformed churches. The other Christians are all tolerated here, but one silences the first that wishes to stir up civil war. I am neutral between Rome and Geneva. Thus I can diminish religious animosities by preaching moderation to all parties, and I try to unite them by reminding them that they are all citizens."

The survey of domestic policy closes with the familiar plea for enlightened autocracy. The prince should rule as well as reign. The public interest is his own. While a minister is apt to think of his career the sovereign concerns himself only with the public interest, supporting the nobility, keeping the clergy in their place, and rewarding merit. Since finance and administration, policy and the army, are indissolubly connected their coordination can only emanate from a single brain, namely that of the sovereign. Indolence, frivolity and folly often prevent princes from securing the happiness of their people. The sovereign is the first servant of the state. . . .

The political treatises of Frederick the Great are the Bible of Enlightened Autocracy. The ruling of a state is presented as the noblest as well as the most onerous of human responsibilities. The Prince must lead a dedicated life, knowing everything, supervising everything, seeing as much as possible with his own eyes. The main difference between these utterances and those of James I, Louis XIV and Bossuet is that religion plays no part and that there is no nonsense about divine right. Every ruler must justify himself by his acts. The author's devotion to the welfare of his subjects shines through his pages, and in the unwearying discharge of his duties he tow-ered above all contemporary rulers. . . .

Like other autocrats, enlightened or unenlightened, he tolerated no opposition to his will. After ordering a caricature of himself to be hung lower so that everybody could see it, he remarked: "Let them say what they like so long as I can do what I like." "Do not talk to me of your liberty of thought and the press," wrote Lessing to Nicolai in 1769. "It is merely permission to attack religion. Let someone raise his voice for the rights of subjects or against exploitation and despotism, and you will soon discover which is the most slavish land in Europe." Wieland declared that while he felt the greatest admiration for the King of Prussia, he thanked heaven that he did not live under his sceptre. When Goethe visited Berlin in 1776 he was disgusted by the abuse of the ruler to which he had to listen. Since the old stoic had too low an opinion of human nature to expect gratitude, he was content to do his duty as he understood it. That there might ever be an alternative to paternalism, any sharing by his subjects in bearing the burden of government, never crossed his mind.

A Royal Reactionary

LEO GERSHOY

In this passage, Gershoy reviews Frederick's reign and assesses his enlightened statements by measuring them against the social consequences of his policies. His verdict is much more critical of the Prussian ruler than that of Gooch.

No OTHER RULER in that age of royal luminaries so aroused the admiration of his contemporaries as Frederick the Great. Posterity remains dazzled, too, by the magnitude of his achievements, and an outstanding liberal among American scholars of our own day could write: "And in everything but his militarism he was the

From Leo Gershoy, *From Despotism to Revolution, 1763–1789* (New York, 1944), pp. 85–89.

most enlightened ruler of his time; his government was the most economical, the most efficient, the most tolerant, and the most progressive then known . . . he made Prussia the most enlightened country in the world." [Preserved Smith]

A decent respect toward his claims to greatness does not preclude an examination of the price of glory, nor does it forbid raising the question of how much he sacrificed of the aggregate good in this attainment of prestige, power, and security for the state. Frederick himself grew old before his time in his struggle with the bureaucracy. Opposing tugs and pulls joined him to the chariot of officialdom, not a oneness of will and direction. The silent obstruction of his functionaries sapped his weak vitality. Even his extraordinary vigilance proved unavailing against intrigues and cabals. Prussian tradition makes the disciplined civil bureaucracy the true builders of the country's unity. These administrators and officers, runs the official version, were the fountainhead of the state's power, paragons of disinterestedness, efficiency, honesty and obedience. These virtues they possessed at least in part, but Frederick's reign also reveals them in a harsher light. They emerge from the recesses of almost mythological greatness as long-suffering, long-complaining, and embittered scribes, secretaries and secret agents, overworked and underpaid functionaries struggling with voluminous reports and batches of memoranda.

To correct their low efficiency, which infuriated him when it did not fill him with dismay, Frederick introduced, as has been seen, a considerable measure of personal supervision. Neither his personality nor his outlook favored the success of his command over subordinate officials. He was incurably, almost pathologically, misanthropic, regarding the bulk of humanity as foolish at best and ferocious at worst. Men were governed, he insisted, by two principal motives: fear of punishment and hope of reward. "The enlightenment," he said, "is a light from heaven for those who stand on the heights, and a destructive firebrand for the masses." Of his own countrymen he wrote doubtlessly with justice but in any case with step-fatherly contempt that they were Brandenburgers and not Englishmen.

As he grew older, his worst qualities came to the fore in the morose and royal neurotic. He chivied and harassed his officials, making his own tours of inspection and relying upon the reports of his secret inspectors, the dreaded fiscals. For a model of administrative efficiency Prussian officialdom presented an astonishingly high total of purges. Toward his associates he was without thanks, gratitude being reserved — as Voltaire once acidly observed — for the horse that carried him away from his first encounter on the battlefield. To his subordinates he was coarse of speech and penurious of purse. He endeavored to improve the efficiency of his officials by the singular expedient of stifling their initiative. But by ruthlessly imposing his own *"Kabinets-Ordres"* upon them he largely impaired their usefulness for tasks other than of his own invention.

The cost to society of this curious blend of personal despotism and institutionalized absolutism was equally high. The officials could not tap a potentially rich vein of individual talent in the local area, for the mass of the population was disbarred from participating and denied a voice in the conduct of local affairs. The townspeople and the villagers detested the royal agents for a dullish fidelity to a state that was remote from them, alien to their expectations, and aloof and unheeding to their wants. It seemed remote and unheeding to them, because the supreme ruler could not minister to their needs. The great increase in agricultural productivity brought no gain to the peasantry. The harsh juridical relations between Junker and peasant were not relaxed. The stupendous expansion of industrial and commercial enterprise under the aegis of a state working largely for the needs of its military machine unquestionably gave a vitalizing shock to the more alert villagers and quickened the capitalistic zeal of the urban entrepreneur. By destroying the old medieval and communal torpor, Frederick's Prussia opened the vistas of boundless opportunities of free enterprise for the resourceful and ambitious. But Frederick thwarted the hopes that he awakened in the capitalist producer. Though the economic changes cleared the way for the disciplined labor force of a later day and prepared the way for the transformation of social power relationship, it was in Frederick's own day, as Treitschke candidly noted, "an unnoticed and an undesirable transformation." Whatever the future relations were to be, for the present the state hemmed producer and production in the strait jacket of regulation and control.

The fiscal arrangements fell heavily upon both producers and consumers. Military needs came first in public finances, for war was indeed the national industry of Prussia. Out of the 22,000,000 or 23,-000,000 thalers of government revenue in 1786, between 12,000,000 and 13,000,000 alone were expended directly to support the huge army of 195,000 men. Even after 60,000,000 thalers had been disbursed between 1763 and 1786 to encourage economic growth, the *Dispositionskasse* still contained a metallic hoard of 52,500,000 thalers when Frederick died. Of the 100,-000,000 or more thalers that were minted during the second half of his reign, only 66,000,000 were in circulation. It is absurd to deny that he began the transformation of Prussia into a modern industrialized state; and it would be equally absurd to deny that the policy of sterilizing money and hoarding specie — which was of a piece with his general mercantilist outlook — seriously retarded a potentially still more rapid extension than took place. He could not raise capital from the public because there were no accumulated savings to be absorbed; and he would not do so because he treated public finance in the manner that a householder considered a family budget, regarding public debt as a liability

instead of the obverse of national investment. There was no great capacity to consume finished products at home, because there was no widely distributed purchasing power. The inherited practice of total or partial tax exemption for the old privileged social groups put the weight of tax liability upon those least qualified to bear it and simultaneously depressed the living standards of the many. Government savings, expenditures on agriculture and industry, and the upkeep of the enormous military establishment all came from the taxes that were efficiently exacted, mainly from the poor. The free-born and free-trading English envoy, Sir James Harris (Lord Malmesbury), got at the root of the matter when he reported in 1776:

The king of Prussia never can be taught to believe that a large treasure laying [sic] dormant in his coffers impoverishes his kingdom; that riches increase by circulation; that trade cannot subsist without reciprocal profit; that monopolies and exclusive grants put a stop to emulation and, of course, to industry; and in short, that the real wealth of a sovereign consists in the ease and affluence of his subjects. These errors, however capital they are, have rather served to augment the misery of these subjects than impede the progress of his own grandeur. . . .

Seen in restrospect the imposing might of militarized Prussia was already hollow when Frederick died. Frederick's Prussia, a military superstructure set upon crumbling foundations, faced the new world that was dawning. It collapsed dramatically during the stress of the Napoleonic wars, because in a world increasingly based upon individual conduct, in a world that was already revolutionary before the upheaval in France, the great Prussian ruler kept its bases unchanged and the ends and purposes of state policy unaltered. An artist like Winckelmann shuddered when he thought of his native "Prussian despotism . . . that scourge of nations," and the cultured Lessing wrote (in a private letter): "Let somebody raise his voice for the rights of subjects or against exploitation, and you will soon see which is the most slavish land in Europe." In a world moving toward the liberating play of bourgeois enterprise and free international exchange, Prussian purposes and ends remained, theory notwithstanding, outmoded and reactionary in practice. To see, as Spengler in an uninspired moment saw, the systematized and militarized statism of Prussia as the point of departure for modern socialism is to twist the meaning of socialism out of all semblance to the original. The great renovation that Frederick quickened could not release the humanist values at the core of the eighteenth-century enlightenment, because he himself was enlightened but not liberal. The Gallic and rococo veneer of his personal surroundings was a thin gloss over a great body of barrack brutality. A wit and a cynic, and at heart a true son of his martinet father, he wove more tightly the pattern of a society that was dying and ably reinforced a structure that required razing. The dynamic ruler was in short a reforming reactionary who propounded solutions for the dilemmas of a new age in terms of remedies that were already outmoded for his own.

The Typical Enlightened Despot

FRITZ HARTUNG

In this continuation of his earlier selection, Hartung tries to place Frederick into the perspective of eighteenth-century politics and to define more exactly his degree of dependence upon the enlightenment. If Frederick was the culminating point of enlightened despotism, he notes, he also demonstrated its limitations.

OF THE MONARCHS who are to be regarded as the typical representatives of enlightened absolutism, I would certainly not wish to include Frederick William I of Prussia . . . or hardly Peter the Great. One should not judge the Prussian king solely by his cabinet order that Christian Wolff leave Prussia or be hanged, But one should also not overestimate the intellectual threads which bound together the work of Frederick William and of Wolff. Frederick William's scorn for scientific knowledge was displayed not only in this cabinet order, but also in his treatment of the Prussian Academy of Sciences . . . In his Instructions for the General Directory, the Prussian king noted with pride that he derived his economic and political precepts from "experience" and not from books. It therefore appears to me to be proper, even today, to begin the series of enlightened despots with Frederick the Great.

His views on the state have been so often and so thoroughly studied that I can add little here that is new. I will dispense with an account of them, especially since Frederick's theories, with their derivation of the state from an original free state of mankind and a social contract, are by no means original. Even his oft-quoted description of the prince as "the first servant of the state" goes back to antiquity. But Frederick was the first monarch who not only used these

From Fritz Hartung, "Der aufgeklärte Absolutismus," Historische Zeitschrift, CLXXX (1955), pp. 26–31. Reprinted by permission of Fritz Hartung and R. Oldenbourg Verlag. Translation by the editor.

words, but put them into practice throughout his government. . . .

His religious policy, which secularized the state . . . freed it from denominational restrictions and allowed everyone to seek salvation in his own way, brought him more fame among his enlightened contemporaries than his military achievements. His attitude toward law and legal procedure was based completely upon the ideas of the Enlightenment. In this sphere, more than any other he was dependent upon the advice of experts, such as Cocceji or Carmer. But the sections in his political testaments on these matters prove that he had thought seriously about these questions and that he recognized the right of the inhabitants of his kingdom to prompt and impartial legal decisions. Frederick's financial administration also shows the influence of enlightened thought, and not merely in particular details. In contrast to his father's practice, he subordinated the interest of the royal treasury to the general interest of the country. This can also be seen in the repeated acknowledgement of the principle that the king was not the owner, but only the administrator of the wealth of the country, and therefore had no right to administer it arbitrarily. How far these ideas conflicted with those of his father can be seen in a comparison of the Royal Domain Edict (1713) of Frederick William I with the similar paragraphs in the *Allgemeine Landrecht* [the codification of Prussian law issued in 1794, but prepared in the closing years of Frederick the Great's reign]. Frederick William I considered the domains as merely a part of the inheritance of the House of Brandenburg, while the *Allgemeine Landrecht* described them as the property of the state from which the monarch was entitled to draw "certain goods and services." Thus the state as a permanent organization is deliberately set above the mortal person of the monarch.

But this is nothing new. The common opinion that the modern state was the private property of the ruler since it was his creation, that ever since Machiavelli the expression "stato" had meant only the monarch and his immediate following, and that only with enlightened despotism did the state come to be seen as a unity of monarch and people — these are untrue generalizations. In the smaller German territories a conception of the state could not develop, because they were too tiny. Nor did such a concept play an important role [in Prussia] for the Great Elector or Frederick William I. But in sixteenth-century France, distinctions were already made between "ordinances of the king" and "ordinances of the kingdom." In the critical year of 1589, Bodin expressly entitled himself "the procurer of the public and of the royal estate, not of the king." This conception of the state was occasionally obscured by the theory of the divine right of kings in seventeenth-century France, but it was never entirely discarded. Even Louis XIV, whose opponents complained that the king counted for everything, and the state counted for nothing in royal policy, not only never uttered the famous words "l'etat c'est moi," but on his deathbed specifically acknowledged these principles of the state. His recently discovered statement was "I pass on, but the state remains forever."

Nonetheless, it remains Frederick's great contribution that he adopted this concept of the sovereign state, and thereby gave to the higher bureaucracy of Prussia an unchangeable standard for their work, so that they could continue the absolute system of government down to 1848, although the leadership of the monarchy weakened after Frederick's death.

The subordination of the ruler to the state did not mean a decrease in the absolute powers of the crown. Even in the *Allgemeine Landrecht* all the rights and duties of the state were vested in the monarch, whose powers of legislation and taxation were not restricted by parliamentary institutions. And the ruler made use of his powers in the spirit of the tutelary police-state which reserved for itself the right to regulate all the external activities of the citizens for the purposes of the state. Although the "natural liberties and rights of the citizens might not be restricted any more than was required by the common purpose," we arrive at this point at the limit which the enlightened despots did not dare to overstep. It was not so much that the principle of authoritarian leadership was maintained, for most of the theoretical writers felt that it must continue until the immature citizen had attained his political maturity. The decisive point is that this leadership did not dare either in the *Allgemeine Landrecht* or in its political administration to attack the existing divisions of society and classes determined by birth. The *Landrecht* recognized that this division had been made obsolete by the development of the modern state. It declared expressly that the laws should apply to "all members of the state without distinction of class, rank, or sex," and that every inhabitant was entitled to the state's protection for his person and property. But it was not thought incompatible with the *Landrecht* to grant to the nobility special advantages over the other classes; to include all laws dealing with business, exchange, maritime and insurance measures under the section entitled: "the Middle Class"; and to maintain fully the nobility's restrictive control of the peasants.

For Frederick, this contradiction between enlightened theory and absolute practice was caused for the most part by the requirements of power politics. Prussia's situation as the youngest and the weakest of the great powers was too precarious for the king to shake his state with the conflicts which would have resulted from a radical break with the traditional agricultural system based on hereditary serfdom. Not only the finances of the state, but also the army would have been affected.

However, alongside this "imperative of political necessity," as Meinecke expressed it, Frederick's own personal character influenced his stopping short of the logical consequences of his own enlightened doctrines. Dilthey once praised Frederick's policy warmly: "this was a prospect un-

paralleled in history, to see how in this Prussian state everyone enthusiastically worked together, king, officers, officials, clergymen, teachers and writers toward a common goal, to educate the people by enlightening them." But it cannot be denied that the personal interest of Frederick in the Prussian school system was very slight, even after 1763, and this was not because of lack of time. He did not trouble himself about the education of the broad mass of people. True, there are some passages in his writings where he declares himself in favor of the spread of enlightenment, or at least denies that it was easier to rule an ignorant people. But deep in his heart he was completely untouched by the joyful optimism of the Enlightenment, which hoped that the spread of knowledge and the fight against prejudice would lead to the moral progress of mankind. On the contrary, he became ever more convinced of the incorrigible evil of the "maudite race" of men. Thus Frederick's own contribution to the development of cultural life in Prussia in the second half of his reign was not so much due to his active encouragement as to the general impetus which he gave, and the fact that he did nothing to hinder or restrict it. Thus for a while Berlin became the center of the Enlightenment in Germany.

But Frederick's personal views had a definitely restrictive influence in the field of economic policy. He did have some ideas on the subject, and the progressive income tax which he proposed in his Political Testament of 1768 was remarkably modern. But we cannot assume that he ever systematically studied economics, and he took no notice at all of the newer ideas of the Physiocrats. An unpublished Berlin dissertation by A. Philippson (1945) establishes in detail the fact that his readings on the subject were very conservative, and that he paid little attention to new publications. In practice, he never departed from the system of mercantilism which he inherited from his father; he may have refined it somewhat, but he did not essentially change it. This meant that he continued to use a system of prohibitive measures to force his subjects to produce at home what they could not import from abroad . . . The question as to whether different times required a different economic policy apparently never occurred to him, although the general application of mercantilistic principles gradually made trade so difficult that everyone suffered by it. And when his ministers cautiously raised the question, he sharply rejected their suggestions, without even considering their arguments.

Frederick's attitude toward the peasantry is especially noteworthy. He was clearly aware of the contradiction between his theory of the original equality of man and of the real situation of the peasants, but he did nothing to change or alleviate things to any significant degree. Even on the royal domain estates, except for a more strict supervision of the tenants, his reforms remained restricted to one major change: the transformation of the precarious tenure of the peasants into hereditary tenure (1777). Nothing at all was done for the peasants who lived on the noble estates. The cabinet order of 1763 had decreed the abolition of serfdom in Pomerania. Despite the strong wording of the draft: "absolutely and without argument," it was never put into effect. The protection which the crown extended to the peasantry was effective only in preventing the nobility from acquiring peasant land — a protection for the peasantry as a whole, not the individual peasant — and this was in the interest of protecting the source of peasant recruits for the army.

It seems to me that this strong attitude of reserve where the welfare of the peasantry was at stake, reveals the importance of Frederick's own personal feeling, which always played a great part in determining his policy. His contempt for the broad masses was joined to an outspoken preference for the aristocracy. He diverted Prussian absolutism away from the line which it had followed since its beginnings under the Great Elector, the repression of the demands of the nobility. It is true that the battle with the aristocracy which Frederick William I had fought with all his energy had become unnecessary, since the nobles had bowed to absolutism and voluntarily taken on the duties of military service as officers. But in the long run, the preference for the nobility which Frederick and nearly all of the Hohenzollern kings exhibited had fateful consequences for the state.

Thus Frederick, with all of his enlightenment, was not a man who opened a new path to the future for his state, but stood at the end of a long line of absolute monarchs. This does not detract in any way from the positive accomplishments of his reign. . . .

Joseph II: Enlightened Reformer

WILHELM TREUE

Currently a professor of history at the Technical University of Hanover, Wilhelm Treue (1909–   ) is the editor of *Tradition*, a journal of business and economic history. He has written studies of economic and cultural history ranging from the eighteenth to the twentieth century, including books on the Crimean War and modern navies. This selection is taken from his survey of German history and gives a traditional picture of Joseph as an enlightened despot who not only based his policies on the ideas of the *philosophes* but went considerably beyond the example of Frederick the Great.

WHEN MARIA THERESA died in 1780, her oldest son, co-regent and now successor Joseph II was almost 40 years old. Now he had the opportunity to realize his reform ideas, ideas which belonged completely to the Enlightenment. His efforts won him, on the one hand, the title of a "crowned friend of man," on the other the criticism of those who saw in him only a rationalist doctrinaire, and an ignorant enemy of tradition and feeling. One cannot deny the seriousness of his efforts, his extraordinary energy, and the fact that he gave his state and people a great stimulus. On the other hand, he was often much too hasty in his efforts to conquer and set aside the middle ages. He proceeded without regard for historical values and the justifiable sentiments of those who thought differently. His conviction that the state should control life, according to standards of reason and ability, led to many erroneous attempts. . . .

As an enlightened despot, his conception of the role of the prince extended the Frederician idea. Aiming to strengthen Austria, he was an energetic centralizer who restricted the influence of the nobility and the self-government of the towns. He revised frontiers, established new fields of government activity and reorganized the administration. The police and the bureaucracy were enlarged and accorded significant rights. Justice was centralized, and new law codes published. In 1786 the first draft of the general law code, and in 1788 of the *Josephina* appeared, markedly more lenient than the criminal provisions of the *Nemesis Theresiana*. This extreme thoroughness led to a stronger and healthier state. After establishing a census, a unified land tax was proclaimed which was based upon natural law and divided the burdens equally among nobles, clergy and peasants. But all the measures proclaimed were never carried out. The mercantilistic economic system was dismantled, along the lines suggested by the Physiocrats. Free ports were established on the Adriatic coast, while an East India Company was organized. Trade agreements were signed with Russia, Turkey and the United States to encourage foreign trade. Austria's economy and its traditional habits of self-sufficiency did not really require such trade, however, and so many of these attempts were never realized, and many of the expectations never fulfilled.

Joseph's most significant measures were promulgated according to the Physiocratic

From Wilhelm Treue, *Deutsche Geschichte von 1713–1806* (Berlin, 1957), pp. 76–82. Reprinted by permission of Walter W. De Gruyter Verlag. Translated by the editor.

idea that the peasantry was the most noble of all the classes, and he carried out the emancipation of the peasants already begun by his mother. In the years 1781–1782 serfdom was abolished in the Austrian-Bohemian lands "as demanded by the laws of nature, and the common good." The peasants were made hereditary tenants of the lands which they farmed. The transformation of the *robot* service and produce payments into money payments, as well as state protection for the peasant from his landlord, sprang from the spirit of Maria Theresa and made possible progress which occurred only partly in Prussia, and not until after 1806. Joseph's efforts to raise the yield of agriculture and to colonize territory in the southeast were also in the same strongly Physiocratic direction. So was the abolition of local courts under the nobility, the raising of the level of culture and handicrafts, and the breakdown of the guilds.

The emperor was especially active in the area of cultural and educational policies. He established modern orphan homes, and insane asylums, introduced seven years of compulsory education, helped the school teachers and overcame a great deal of pedantic resistance to the practical and utilitarian. Among these efforts was also the establishment of the *Burgtheater* in 1776 as a "national theatre," a concept developed by Joseph Sonnenfels. . . .

But rationalism and a narrow state-mindedness . . . often led to an excessively restricted view. In carrying out the secularization of the high schools and the universities short-sighted goals were established, limiting the education of civil servants chiefly to administration and economics. In place of the ecclesiastical censorship, state censorship was established. This aided the supporters of Josephinism . . . but the broad generosity so essential to a deep intellectual and literary flowering was lacking. Here, as in many other areas, enlightenment and *raison d'état* came into conflict. Usually the demands of the state won out although the measures appear dressed in modern clothing.

The Tolerance Edict of 1781 which caused such commotion did proclaim religious freedom, but in practice was less important. The Catholic religion expressly maintained its preeminence in the interest of the unity of the state. This same outlook of the independence and power of the state also explained the fight against any papal influence. State approval was required for publication of papal bulls and letters, the higher clergy was put under the strict supervision of the government, connections of religious orders with their foreign organizations dissolved, and contemplative and ascetic monasteries were declared useless and unpleasing to God. The property and income from dissolved monasteries was used to create a Religious Fund for the education of a better trained clergy more loyal to the state . . . Processions and pilgrimages were banned, elaborate ceremonies for funerals and other events reduced; according to the official explanation, because they were unreasonable, and hindered real devotion; actually, to emphasize the power of the state.

Pope Pius VI attempted to halt this policy by a visit to Vienna in 1782, but he failed because of Joseph's resistance. Kaunitz treated the Pope merely as an equal prince, and managed not only to keep Joseph from making any concessions, but on the Pope's departure placed the whole property of the church under state control. . . .

The whole policy called Josephinism had many goals in common with the movement in Catholic Germany called Febronianism. The latter grew out of the book "On the State of the Church and the Legitimate Powers of the Roman Pontiff" published in 1763 under the pseudonym of Justinus Febronius (the auxiliary bishop of Trier, Nicholas Hontheim, one of a group influenced by Gallicanism). It demanded a sharp delimitation of the authority of the Pope and the reunion of the Christian denominations. The book was chiefly influential in reviving the medieval idea of conciliarism, which sought to prevent absolutism in the church, and in its suggestion that bishops work most closely with the secular governmental authorities. Though Hontheim recanted his ideas in 1776, in the meantime a movement had formed which was led by the Rhenish Elector-Archbishops. Protestantism took only a literary part in the controversy. This led to strong conflict between the Pope and the German Archbishops of Mainz, Trier, Cologne and Salzburg. Joseph II denied that the papal Nuncio had any jurisdiction, and in 1786 the Ems Punctuation [a manifesto by the German archbishops] led to the formulation of a large scale church reform. But it soon became apparent that the reform-minded higher clergy had only a small following among the lesser bishops and the secular princes, who saw that the movement directed against the Pope . . . would also affect their own sovereignty. Even Joseph II finally declined to call an anti-Roman National Council. In the end, the reformers became divided among themselves, so this "last attempt to form a *Reichskirche*" collapsed. At the same time, Josephinism entered into a serious crisis. The forces of tradition in religion and politics banded together with representatives of aristocratic self-government to revolt in favor of local liberties and historical traditions, and against "despotic benevolence and centralistic order."

Hungary, whose Crown of St. Stephen Joseph had carted off to Vienna as a museum piece, and whose strength he had increased by the annexation of Transylvania, refused to become part of the emperor's planned centralized state. In the Netherlands revolution broke out for the same reasons in 1787, when it became known that Joseph degraded the land to the status of an object of exchange, and finally introduced the Austrian centralization. In 1789, two weeks before the storming of the Bastille, he revoked the ancient charter of liberties, the *Joyeuse Entrée* (which contained the right of resistance against unjust

rulers) at the same time that the international situation appreciably worsened.

In the face of such resistance, the rapidly aged emperor saw himself forced on his deathbed in early 1790 to repeal part of his measures. He had tried in vain to decree great reforms from above, while at the same time new and to him inconceivable middle class ideas of freedom rose up from below. Nonetheless, the reforms of Joseph II continued to exercise an influence on the clergy and bureaucracy until the middle of the nineteenth century. [Joseph II] was personally unpretentious, an extremely hard working idealist, but also a proud and cold-hearted prince, and his personality naturally remains disputed even today, praised by liberals and especially criticized in clerical circles. If Josephinism was unsuccessful during the emperor's lifetime, it was because of the excessive haste with which the reforms were put into effect. Also, the reforms were designs based more upon theory than upon actual conditions, and Joseph's desire to introduce them all simultaneously unified all his opponents, whose resistance could have been crushed singly by the state . . . Joseph's foreign policy, especially the Turkish war of 1788–1791, took an unfortunate course. . . .

Joseph attempted more than did Frederick the Great; but in contrast he was a less important statesman. He did not know exactly the powers and tendencies of his own people (though he needed to) and as a result did not achieve as much. He left behind him a weaker, and even less unified state, and even eroded the foundations of his own throne. According to Srbik, "he tried to reshape historically developed Austria into a mechanical western state rationalism. He drove enlightened absolutism to its despotic peak . . . made centralism overreach itself and in his political fanaticism failed to appreciate intellectual and artistic culture. . . ."

Joseph II: Determined by Circumstances

ERNST WANGERMANN

Ernst Wangermann is a British historian who has taught modern European history at the University of Leeds, and has written the section on Germany and Austria in the period after 1763 for the *New Cambridge Modern History*. The following is taken from his study of the reaction against Josephinism which culminated in the Austrian Jacobin trials of 1794. Like other recent historians such as Lefebvre and Morazé, Wangermann emphasizes the underlying economic and social factors. He concludes that enlightened despotism in Austria arose to meet practical needs, and not as a result of philosophical theory, and points out that it led to some consequences not foreseen by Joseph II.

MANY PHILOSOPHERS wrote with the aim of converting rulers. Many philosophers of the eighteenth century believed that they had succeeded. Some lived to be disillusioned.

The apparent conversion was in fact due to purely practical considerations. Many governmental policies which have commonly been regarded as the fruits of the prevailing enlightened philosophy may be interpreted more convincingly as the appropriate eighteenth-century form of the general policy of centralizing and strengthening the State, attempted by monarchs in western Europe since the thirteenth century.

Since the development of the Atlantic trade routes, the countries sharing the Atlantic seaboards had been in the vanguard of economic advancement, and therefore of political centralization. The countries of central and eastern Europe, far away from the new trading centres and afflicted by invasion from primitive and savage nations, remained backward in comparison until the end of the seventeenth century. At about that time, able monarchs in Russia and Brandenburg-Prussia embarked on a policy of state centralization and expansion by importing artificially some at least of the economic development which had made England, Spain, and France powerful. The growing strength and the expansion of Russia and Prussia caused alarm and forced the pace in the Habsburg dominions. The loss of Silesia to Prussia in 1740 was a symptom of the ominous fact that the Habsburgs had fallen behind in the European rulers' race for strength. The greatness of the Empress Maria Theresa lies in the fact that she was prepared to take all necessary steps to remedy this situation, however strongly these might conflict with her personal inclinations.

The Empress was determined to regain Silesia in a new trial of strength. This determination was the starting-point of the great series of reforms which is associated with her name and that of her son Joseph. A beginning was made with the reform of the armed forces. This implied reforms in other fields: the maintenance of the new armed forces required a substantial increase in taxation which, in turn, could be obtained only by constitutional, political, economic, and administrative reforms of the most far-reaching order. To put the reforms into effect, a new civil service was

From Ernst Wangermann, *From Joseph II to the Jacobin Trials* (Oxford, 1959), pp. 1–4. Reprinted by permission of the Clarendon Press, Oxford.

required, and to train the civil servants, a new educational system freed from clerical control and censorship had to be built up.

A policy of enlightened despotism thus appeared in Austria no less than elsewhere in response to certain practical and urgent necessities, and not as the fruit of philosophical persuasion. The statement is as valid for the reign of Joseph II as it is for that of his mother. The "revolutionary" Emperor undertook little that was entirely new in principle. But his obstinate consistency and enthusiasm has always provided historians with an additional temptation to impute philosophical motives to him, which has resulted in a long-standing and sterile controversy as to the theoretical origin of his reforms.

It does not, of course, follow that the philosophy and political theory of the eighteenth century is irrelevant to the study of enlightened despotism. The philosophers and their disciples played a role in the practical application of the enlightened despots' policies which was neither insignificant nor without consequences. They were mistaken in their belief that they had converted the despots. But it was an unmistakable resemblance between many of the reforms and the principles they were advocating that gave rise to their illusion. The resemblance symptomized a certain limited conformity of interest between the monarchy and the classes for whom the philosophers of the Enlightenment were speaking. To increase its financial resources, the absolute monarchy needed a more numerous and prosperous capitalist class. To combat the short-sighted opposition of aristocracy and clergy against the curtailment of their privileges, it had to bring up behind its lines the ideological cannon of middle-class anti-aristocratic and anti-clerical philosophers, journalists, and university professors. To implement the vast programme of far-reaching reforms, it had to rely on the initiative and enthusiasm of the graduate civil servants trained by the latter.

In this way the reforms of enlightened despotism helped to awaken the non-privileged classes in the Habsburg dominions from their political slumber and to bring them, for the first time since the Reformation, into the field of political action. Not all the consequences of such a political renaissance had, however, been foreseen by Joseph II, and some of them alarmed him and his successors acutely. For the political struggle of the Fourth Estate transcended fairly quickly the limits marked out by official instructions and encouragement. By the end of Joseph II's reign, the non-privileged classes had gained enough at the expense of the privileged to desire more; enough, in fact, to envisage, however vaguely, complete social and political emancipation.

So far was this from the intentions of Joseph II, that we may regard it as among the decisive factors leading ultimately to the abandonment of enlightened despotism by the Habsburg monarchy. The more timid elements in the Fourth Estate relapsed into a disillusioned inactivity. The rest, encouraged by the news from France after 1789, found themselves inevitably driven into opposition to the monarchy itself. The monarchy, now thoroughly frightened, embarked on the political suppression of its former allies whom it had so recently strengthened and encouraged, but now found to be infected with the "fever of freedom" and the poison of "Jacobinism."

Catherine as Enlightened Empress

MELVIN C. WREN

Melvin C. Wren (1910–   ) a professor of Russian History at Montana State University, describes in this selection the reform work of Catherine the Great and gives a positive evaluation of her reign. Catherine's liberal plans date chiefly from the early period of her reign, and many historians see a change in emphasis in her policy after the Pugachev serf rebellion of 1773. She was highly critical of the French Revolution. In his account of Catherine's reform achievements, Wren also notes that most of them benefited the gentry rather than the mass of the serf population.

CATHERINE II (1762–1796), whose fawning admirers called her the Great, considered herself the heir and executor of the reforms of Peter the Great. Unlike Peter, however, whose reforms were thoroughly practical if seldom thought through, Catherine was doctrinaire in the reforms which she conceived. They were planned in the spirit of enlightened despotism of which Catherine was a devotee and a classic example. . . .

Catherine's greatest achievements were in adding territory to the state and in reducing or eliminating the threat to Russian security posed by neighbors to the west and south. Two successful wars against Turkey carried the Russian border to the Black Sea and west to the Dniester river. Most ominous for the future peace of the Ottoman Empire and for Europe, Russia obtained the right, vaguely stated, to interfere in the domestic affairs of Turkey on behalf of Christians living under the sultan's rule. Catherine planned, but failed, to rid the European continent of Turkish power and even to revive the Byzantine Empire as a sort of Russian protectorate. . . .

. . . Like Peter I, she did not abandon herself to sensuality as had some of her immediate predecessors. She worked hard and conscientiously at the job of governing Russia personally, not through favorites, and went to her lovers almost by way of seeking relaxation from strenuous toil. She began the day at six, an unheard-of hour for Russian officials in any age, lit her own fire, spent little time before the mirror, and worked twelve or fifteen hours a day. Like Peter the Great, who considered himself the first servant of the state, Catherine labored more diligently than any other person in the government.

The extent of her knowledge and her appetite for reading made her one of the best-read women in Europe and the most unusual and outstanding woman in Elizabethan Russia. For that reason, among others, she much preferred the companionship of men and prided herself on her ability to converse and correspond, as an equal in many cases, with the best minds of her day. Voltaire, whose sincerity is hardly open to question in spite of the fact that he received generous gifts from her, was one of her most uncritical admirers. Diderot was her pensioner and visited Russia to become a keen admirer of her remarkable gifts both as a woman and as an intellectual. She corresponded at great length with Frederick II, Joseph II, Gustavus II, and with D'Alembert, Falconnet, Grimm, and others

From Melvin C. Wren, *The Course of Russian History* (New York, 1958), pp. 293–304. Reprinted by permission of The Macmillan Company. Copyright © by The Macmillan Company 1958.

of the encyclopedists, of whom both she and they considered her one. She read Plato, Tacitus, Blackstone, Buffon, Montesquieu, Rousseau, Bayle, and Beccaria, as well as the *Encyclopédie* which fascinated her. . . .

Steeped in Western liberal thought, determined not to dilute her autocratic power but to use it for the benefit of her subjects, Catherine conceived an ambitious plan to provide the nation with a new law code which would reflect Western humanitarian principles. There had been no revision of the Russian code since 1649. There were at least ten thousand laws on the books, many of them contradictory or obscure or hopelessly out of date. . . .

Catherine decided to convoke a great national commission of elected delegates to work out the principles upon which a new law code could be based. To give direction to their deliberations the empress herself worked for two years on a *Nakaz*, or set of instructions. Finally the remarkable volume was published, not only in Russia to guide those who would sit on the commission, but abroad as well, where its daring acceptance of liberal principles delighted reformers and shocked conservatives. Louis XV forbade its distribution in France, but Frederick II expressed his approval by making the empress a member of the Berlin Academy. Voltaire compared her to Solon.

Catherine's *Nakaz*, written with her own hand but considerably modified by her advisers, contained twenty chapters and over five hundred paragraphs suggesting principles to which the enlightened state should adhere in politics, economics, social welfare, culture, and religion. More than half of the statements were taken straight out of Montesquieu's *Spirit of the Laws* or Beccaria's *Crime and Punishment;* the empress quickly admitted as much. But there was something of Catherine in it, too — of her ignorance of Russian society, of her naïve assumption that principles worked out tortuously over centuries in other countries could be transplanted, of her supreme confidence in absolutism. The final draft

was stripped, at the prompting of serf-owning advisers, of suggestions that the lot of Russian serfs should be improved. Catherine gave way — spinelessly, her critics charge — before the insistence of court nobles that there be no hint of emancipation or even of the right of a serf to buy his freedom. Her apologists point out that she had no right to the throne, that she owed her accession to the support of the nobles who might easily unseat her by withdrawing that support.

Even with all the editing Catherine meekly accepted, the "Instructions" retained much Western liberal thought that was far in advance of most governments of the time. The *Nakaz* declared that all subjects should be equal before the law; all should obey the law; the state should aim less at the punishment than at the prevention of crime; torture should be abolished and capital punishment resorted to only rarely; serfdom could be justified only if it served the state, but to sweep away bondage at a stroke would be rash and dangerous; all men should be free to do whatever the law does not specifically proscribe; religious dissent ought to be tolerated; the right to own land should be widely encouraged. No nation in Europe practiced or even accepted the validity of all these ideas, and few on the continent practiced any of them.

Catherine unquestionably believed the propositions put forward in the *Nakaz*. But Catherine was a true benevolent despot. There was no hint that these high-minded principles should operate through a representative assembly. Rather, they should guide the sovereign, who would retain in his own hands the full power of absolute monarchy, the only sensible type of government for a land as sprawling as Russia. "The ruler is the source of all civil and political power," according to the *Nakaz*. But that power must be used wisely and justly with the welfare of the people in view. The *Nakaz* also laid down the principle that "the people do not exist for the ruler but the ruler for the people."

The instructions were scattered widely

over Russia, and six months later Catherine called for the election of delegates to a "Legislative Commission" whose assignment was to draft a new law code. In the summer of 1767 over five hundred elected representatives gathered in the Kremlin in Moscow. . . .

The Legislative Commission held over two hundred sessions and innumerable committee meetings. Many of the speeches were less constructive than complaining. Some of the nobles from old families resented the intrusion into their class of those who became gentry through Peter's Table of Ranks. The merchants resented the loss of their trade monopoly and the growing threat of competition from serf-manned factories on landowners' estates. Commoners resented the gentry's monopoly of the right to own serfs, and merchants and Cossacks appealed for the same right.

There were a few constructive suggestions along with the selfish demands. Dmitry Golitsyn's plea at the time of Anne's succession for a legislative assembly and constitutional restrictions on the autocratic power was revived. Several enlightened nobles appealed for a reduction of the landowner's authority over his serfs or at least for a definition of serf rights so that abuses might be punished. Such men were jeered for betraying their own class.

The accomplishments of the Legislative Commission were disappointing. Not even a beginning was made on a new code. The meetings adjourned without even completing the reading of the fifteen hundred statements of grievances brought by the delegates. The debates, however, were a source of information to the empress. Some of the things she learned there helped her in defining some of the later reforms.

From the moment of her accession Catherine felt a responsibility to carry on the reforming work of Peter the Great. Within a month of her husband's death she was busy annulling his edict secularizing church estates. There was no sense or reason behind her action; perhaps she assumed the secularization to be somehow wrong be-

cause Peter III had ordered it. Early in 1764, however, she changed her mind and again confiscated the lands of the church, putting their administration under the Economic College as her predecessor had done. The clergy and the few monasteries not closed received their income from the state.

There were a few minor alterations in the machinery of the central government. During her first Turkish war Catherine created an Imperial Council to advise her on war policy and foreign affairs. The council continued to function, always under the strong hand of the empress, to the end of the century. She abolished most of the colleges and turned their functions over to new local agencies which were responsible, for a while at least, to the Senate. The Admiralty, the Army and the Department of Foreign Affairs were the only colleges to survive. The functions of colleges which had dealt with collection of revenue and the administration of justice were assumed by the procurator-general, who was removed from his earlier contact with the Senate and made a separate and powerful official. This abolition of some offices and transfer of duties from one agency to another was so confusing that when Alexander I later asked the senators what their duties were they were not sure of the answer.

Catherine's reforms in the area of local government were more impressive. Peter the Great had despaired of developing much governmental initiative on the local level when he found there were not enough capable and intelligent men to staff local administrative offices. That such was the case was primarily due to the obligation of every member of the gentry to serve in the armed forces, leaving no one in the provinces to accept civil assignment. The situation altered quickly after Peter's death, however, when most of the gentry shirked their service responsibilities with impunity and returned to their estates. Then Peter III freed the gentry entirely from their obligations.

By a succession of orders between 1764 and 1785 Catherine refined the system of local government which Peter had barely begun. The number of provinces was increased to fifty, each supposed to contain three or four hundred thousand inhabitants. Each province was divided into districts of from twenty to thirty thousand inhabitants each. A governor named by the crown was responsible to the Senate for the administration of each province. However, a number of administrative functions — finance, police, and social welfare — were assigned to provincial boards who were responsible not to the governor but in most cases to the procurator-general's office in St. Petersburg. Civil and criminal courts in the provinces were also accountable to the procurator-general. All these provincial officials were appointed, the governor typically from a well-to-do and influential noble family, the others from the lesser and poorer gentry. The effect of this reorganization of local government was not to promote self-government but to improve the machinery for carrying out the will of the sovereign. Whether this was Catherine's intention may be argued, but that this was the consequence is beyond question.

The gentry of each district and each province received the privilege of electing delegates to a district or provincial assembly which met every three years. The assembly, within certain limits, voted assessments for local needs and elected a "marshal of the nobility," the district assembly on the district level and the province on the provincial level. The provincial or district marshal had to be a person of some influence and dignity, for it was he who had to plead the needs of the nobles before the provincial governor or the appropriate official, sometimes even the tsar, in St. Petersburg. . . .

The gentry received complete freedom from irritating restraints and from all obligations to the state in Catherine's Charter of the Nobility, proclaimed in 1785. The rights granted by Peter III's emancipation of the gentry were not only repeated but

considerably increased. The charter relieved the nobles of all responsibility to enter the military or civil service of the state. They could not be subjected to corporal punishment and were exempted from payment of direct taxes. The life, estates, or title of a noble could not be taken from him except by the verdict of his peers, and he could not be stripped of his title even by court sentence without the approval of the ruler. If, by court sentence, he were deprived of his estates, they went to one of his heirs and could not be seized by the state. None but the gentry could own serf-populated lands, and none but they were free to travel abroad. They could maintain factories on their estates and sell the products, thus sharing the trade rights of the merchants without having to pay the merchants' fees.

By the terms of *ukazes* issued at various times during the century and by unwritten privileges tacitly admitted by the sovereign, the gentry won almost unlimited control over their serfs. They could sell or give away their bondsmen singly or in families, with or without land. They could move serfs out of the village and off the land into their manor houses at will. They could send any serf to the army for the twenty-five-year enlistment period, which the masses looked upon as a life sentence to penal servitude, or exile him to Siberia, which one out of four never reached because so many died along the way. The landowner could subject his serf to unlimited floggings; while he could not condemn his serf to death he could order as many strokes of the lash as he pleased, and he went unpunished if the man or woman died of the beating. Peter the Great had held the gentry accountable — even to the loss of their estates — for abusing their serfs, but this restraint was not enforced after his death. In Peter's time serfs might petition the tsar against mistreatment by their owners, but such complaints were forbidden by Catherine.

The privately-owned serf had no enforceable rights whatever. Had the law recognized any rights, the courts, manned by members of the gentry, would never have enforced them against the landowners. The gentry-owned serfs, who made up over half the nation's population, could not own property, real or even personal. The very rags they wore and the miserable huts they lived in were legally the property of the noble who owned them. Their labor and their earnings were at the disposal of the estate owner.

Villagers living on farming estates customarily owed the landlord three days of work each week, called *barshchina,* on that part of the arable land which the estate owner cultivated for his own use. Ideally, half of the arable land was assigned to the serfs, whose village elders allotted in each field strips on which a serf family could raise its own food. But many a landowner, particularly in the rich black-soil area, forced his serfs to work in the fields five or six days a week, adding the villagers' fields to his own and doling out to them whatever food was necessary to keep them alive. In the gray-soil area of central Russia a landlord might take his fields out of cultivation and work his serfs in factories on the estate. Or he might let his bondsmen farm the land on their own in return for their paying him an annual *obrok,* a money payment in lieu of labor. Or he might let them work in a nearby town and pay the *obrok* out of whatever wages they received. Where the *barshchina* serfs worked under the lash in the landlord's fields and suffered constant interference in their daily lives from the bailiff of the estate, the *obrok*-payers were left free to govern themselves and to use their time as they chose as long as the village saw that each serf paid his *obrok.*

While Catherine did nothing to help landowners' serfs, she certainly improved the lot of state-owned serfs by making them all *obrok*-payers instead of *barshchina* serfs. Left to govern themselves in their own village assemblies, and enjoying generous land allotments, they were much better off than privately-owned serfs and were commonly known as peasants rather than serfs. Whatever rights they enjoyed, however, they possessed only by sufferance of the state, which was a milder, or perhaps merely less efficient and less grasping, landlord than were many nobles. Some state peasants suffered during Catherine's reign, however, for the empress gave away hundreds of thousands of them to her favorites. The reign is commonly looked upon as a period when the lot of the peasants reached its lowest point, for the control of the landowners over their serfs was refined in full detail and whatever rights the privately-owned serfs had previously retained were legally swept away. And millions more peasants were depressed into serfdom as bondage was extended to the Baltic provinces, the Ukraine, and to that part of the Polish-Lithuanian lands which Catherine acquired where serfdom did not already exist.

Peter's efforts to establish municipal government had met with little success beyond the capital. In a 1785 Charter to the Towns Catherine announced a new basis for self-government in the nation's cities. Each city's population was grouped in six categories — owners of real estate, native merchants, foreign merchants, craftsmen, unskilled workers, and "eminent citizens," a catch-all group containing bankers, officials, and university graduates. The city elected a mayor and a duma, or council, which would meet every three years, presumably to decide broad policy matters. In the intervals between its meetings a committee of six, one from each of the corporate groups into which the citizens were divided, was supposed to sit regularly to guide the city administration and to levy taxes. The mayor was responsible to the provincial governor for his administration, as was the head of the local police, who was an appointed, not an elected, official. For most Russian cities, however, Catherine's proposed municipal self-government never went beyond the paper stage. A confusion of appointed officials maintained order and collected taxes until the last half of the nineteenth century. Town inhabitants were exempted from payment of the soul tax which was the exclusive privilege of the "souls" living on state-owned or private estates.

Some new towns came into existence during Catherine's reign. The government claimed to have built nearly a hundred and fifty of them, scattered the breadth of the land from the Arctic to the Black Sea. In 1787, accompanied by a following of Western ambassadors and, most notably, by the Austrian Emperor Joseph II, Catherine went "on progress" down the Dnieper and into the Crimea to view the accomplishments of her government in the land so recently under Turkish rule. Her former lover, Prince Gregory Potemkin, now governor of the area, carefully planned the itinerary and built a number of cities along the way in which the empress was greeted with happy, dancing townsmen in holiday dress. But, in some instances at least, there really were no towns, only false fronts of buildings hastily thrown up like stage settings to impress Catherine and her party. The "Potemkin villages" may have pleased the empress at the time, for she was not privy to the deception, but word of their nature soon leaked out and brought the derision of all Europe.

Catherine encouraged foreigners to settle in the thinly populated lands of the empire, allowing them tax exemptions and freedom to practice their religion in the hope that they would set Russians an example of industry and improved farming methods. Over a hundred colonies of Germans settled in the lower Volga and the Ukraine, jealously clinging to their language and customs until the middle of the twentieth century.

There was a modest approach to *laissez-faire* principles in the economic policies of the government under Catherine. The monopolies which Peter the Great had granted to encourage Russia's infant industries were removed. Tariffs were scaled down to encourage competition. Foreigners were invited into the country to establish factories under preferred conditions, even enjoying the privilege of buying serfs to man their plants, a right which Russian merchants were no longer allowed. The elimination of the monopoly privileges of Russian merchants, however, was a blessing primarily to the gentry, who obtained the right to build factories on their estates and even to sell their products.

In spite of the steady rise in prices brought about by large issues of paper rubles, Russia's foreign trade volume increased markedly during the reign. The government arranged commercial treaties with Western nations, stimulated imports by moderate tariffs, and built or expanded seaports through which the goods could flow. Odessa was founded shortly before Catherine's death, and the empress had visions of a thriving Black Sea trade through the Bosporus, which she hoped Russia might someday control. But not until the latter part of the nineteenth century would the traffic through the southern sea exceed that through the Baltic ports which Peter had done so much to promote.

Catherine made a beginning on a national system of lay schools. Two-year elementary schools were proposed for every district in every province, although many of them never opened and a few closed for want of teachers, students, or funds. Four-year "high" schools were operating in most of the important cities of European Russia by the end of the reign. The government established a teachers' college to produce the teachers with which to staff its new schools. By 1790 sixteen thousand students were enrolled in lay and church schools out of a population of twenty-six million —a pitifully small percentage, but still a beginning. Most of the students came from middle-class homes, for serfs had no time for such frills and the gentry employed private tutors. There were still no schools of any kind in the villages, which meant that at least half the nation's population had no educational facilities.

The empress founded a school for orphans in St. Petersburg and another in Moscow, and she opened the Smolny Institute in the capital as a finishing school for daughters of the gentry. Most sons of the gentry obtained their education either at the officers' schools founded by Peter or from French tutors. They learned to read the works of the French radicals of the time whose writings were popular at court and influential among the nobility throughout this reign and that of Catherine's grandson, Alexander I.

Catherine organized a college of medicine at the University of Moscow. It had graduated only one student by the end of the century, for most Russian medical students sought their education abroad. She set her people an example of confidence in new medical practices by being the first to be vaccinated against smallpox, the scourge of the villages. And she encouraged the health authorities to use quarantine and to forbid the kissing of icons when the plague swept over South Russia during the Turkish war. She ordered the building of a public library in St. Petersburg. She organized the Free Economic Society to stimulate interest in Russian agricultural development. In its first year the society offered a prize to the citizen of any country who should submit the best essay on the problem of serfdom. The winner, a resident of Aix-la-Chapelle, suggested abolition of serfdom. He received the prize, but the society, most of whose members were nobles, refused to publish his essay. They were willing to discuss social theories among themselves, but refused to broadcast this concrete proposal for the alteration of the social order from which they drew so much profit.

The Catherinian reforms differed from those of Peter the Great in one fundamental way. Peter did not pretend that his reforms were carefully thought out or that they were based upon any philosophical precepts. Often they came at the spur of the moment with little regard for their consequences. Almost invariably Peter's reforms were of the practical sort, unadorned with philosophical falderal to lend them dignity. On the other hand, Catherine's reforms, which with few exceptions were much less substantial and much less enduring than Peter's, were conceived and justified in the spirit of enlightenment which was the fad of the age. The empress was proud, if not vain, of her correspondence with other enlightened despots and philosophers and was most anxious to be known abroad as one of such people. She did her best to cultivate among Westerners the belief that Russia was a Western, a European nation and, beyond that, that Russia was particularly prosperous and contented under Catherine's rule. Catherine was always concerned with what people thought of her and Russia. Peter cared little about what others thought as long as he could whip the nation to a level of achievement which would satisfy him and, more important, satisfy Russia's own needs. But it was Catherine, and not Peter, who set the intellectual tone of modern Russia. If Russian merchants and industrialists looked westward in Peter's time, it was the Russian intellectual who looked westward from Catherine's time onward.

The Darker Side of Catherine's Reign

R. D. CHARQUES

Richard Dennis Charques (1899–   ) an English author, critic and historian, has long been interested in aspects of Russian life. He is the author of *The Twilight of Imperial Russia* and *A Short History of Russia*, a careful popular summary of Russian history. Charques emphasizes the interaction of the royal autocracy and the peasant masses as a main theme in the story of Russia's development; the reign of Catherine becomes for him a significant turning point. But it is not the turning point of Wren: Russia's opening to western culture. Rather, Charques notes, it initiated the "irremediable worsening of the condition of the peasantry." Like Frederick the Great, Catherine only appeared to be enlightened, while following reactionary social policies.

No PERIOD of Russian history is comparable in outward splendour with the age of Catherine the Great. This is the spectacular age of St. Petersburg, the golden age of the nobility, the legendary age of Russian opulence and glitter. For the privileged enclave in society who had experienced its *douceur de vivre* the memories of the reign awoke ever afterwards a passion of regret. In extravagance and ostentation the life of the court, duplicated on a smaller scale in the palaces of the aristocracy, was a match for Versailles. It was almost a match also in intellectual polish and pretension. The great figures in society, who drew upon the seemingly inexhaustible wealth of their estates for the luxury they imported from Europe, took their cue from the imperial votary of European enlightenment and followed Catherine in her addiction to the liberal thought of the *philosophes*.

To this cultivation of aristocratic splendour and intellectual freedom was joined an enveloping pride of empire. Russian territorial aggrandizement in Catherine's reign was greater than in any reign since Ivan the Terrible. By war and diplomacy Russia advanced her frontiers in the south and west to what were almost the ultimate limits of expansion in Europe, absorbing in the one direction the Crimea, the Black Sea steppe and its northern shore, in the other the predominantly Russian provinces of Poland together with Courland. Simultaneously Russian settlement spread more widely through the vast spaces of Siberia. The age had its greatness, indeed, whatever Catherine's personal title to greatness may have lacked.

Yet the brilliant surface of achievement, as so often in Russian history, barely disguised the accumulation of decay. All the glitter of the age was paid for in an aggravation of existing evils. Whatever the sentiments she derived from Voltaire, in the dubious circumstances in which she came to the throne Catherine had no choice but to court the favour of the emancipated nobility. The alliance she struck with them left intact all the prerogatives of autocracy, but for their part it enabled the nobility to stretch authority over their peasants to the point at which they themselves were enthroned as local autocrats. Serfdom was never more inhuman in Russia than in the reign of Catherine the Great. It was extended throughout her dominions, and

From R. D. Charques, *A Short History of Russia* (London, 1956), pp. 105–106, 116–118. Reprinted by permission of David Higham Associates, Ltd.

more particularly to the whole of the Ukraine, the Don country and large areas of the Caucasus, by the enormous grants of state land, with its free or semi-free peasants, which she made to her favourites and followers. Catherine's liberalism, in brief, stopped short at affairs of state. Even as a speculative exercise it could not easily survive the Pugachev rebellion in 1773–4 and was finally extinguished by the French Revolution.

Like other enlightened despots among her contemporaries, the empress of Russia enjoyed play-acting. Enlightenment in Catherine was, indeed, not much deeper than her vanity; despotism, on the other hand, was implicit in her ambition. Frederick the Great, notoriously shrewd in these matters, described her as very ambitious and very vain. Vanity was only too evident in her profession of advanced opinions, in her tireless correspondence with the great intellectual figures of the day, in her purchase of Diderot's library for the Hermitage palace, in her own versatile but unoriginal authorship. For all her liveliness of mind and astute grasp of affairs Voltaire's "Semiramis of the North" is above all else an egotist who wishes to be flattered. Even her commanding gifts in administration and diplomacy were furbished with theatrical little tricks of self-advertisement. And vanity entered largely into her appetites. . . .

In the perspective of history, not diplomacy or empire or the brilliance of the age gives the reign of Catherine decisive significance. The future to which it points is shaped rather by the irremediable worsening of the condition of the peasantry. From now onwards no agreed and practicable solution of the fundamental problems of serfdom is in sight. Proposals for reform will multiply, reform itself will extinguish serfdom; but the evils have gone too deep, the difficulties have grown too intractable, to give the liberal forces in society a fair opportunity.

At the end of the reign Russia had a population of 36 million, the largest of any state in Europe. It had increased threefold in the seventy years since the death of Peter the Great, partly through territorial acquisition but in the main by natural increase. Of these 36 million it is estimated that 34 million were peasants, of whom nearly 20 million were serfs on private estates; the remainder, state or crown land peasants, were not far removed from the strict condition of serfdom. As yet the growth of population pressed heavily upon the means of subsistence only in the central regions. Agriculture almost everywhere was still primitive, regulated for the most part by the three-field system, with open fields divided among the peasant households in the village in the traditional pattern of long, narrow strips, and the use of a light wooden plough (*sokha*) that only scratched the surface of the soil. Estates, especially those of larger size, were often mere *latifundia*; the rich owner lived in St. Petersburg, the poorer in the provincial capital, both as rack-rent landlords. On the majority of estates the serfs might number anything from a hundred to a thousand. But the age was noted for its fabulously rich serf-owners, many of them the special recipients of Catherine's bounty, and there were scores who were only a degree less blessed than the Count Sheremetev who possessed 300,000 serfs. Serf dues in rent (*obrok*) commonly consisting of both cash and kind, were the rule in the north, in the less fertile areas which had once been the property of the state; labour dues (*barshchina*) were the normal payment in the black-earth areas and were most often fixed at three days in the week. But it was here, under the stimulus of the expanding trade in grain, that the owners had grown most exacting, the labour dues on many estates having been extended to as much as six days in the week.

Into these varying degrees of economic slavery, to which the payment of state taxes added a growing burden, there entered a deepening moral degradation. The everyday conditions of existence for the peasantry steadily became more brutalized in the golden age of the nobility. The discipline of serfdom was maintained more than all else by corporal punishment; never was the practice of flogging in Russia so extensive, never was the knout considered so sovereign a remedy for peasant failings. Against the injustice or the barbarity of punishment inflicted by his master the peasant had, in effect, no redress. In 1767, almost at the very moment when Catherine had presented her enlightened Instruction for the guidance of the Legislative Assembly, an imperial decree prohibited all complaints by a serf against his master under threat of the severest penalties. Already, indeed, the serf-owner was equipped with the legal right to punish a peasant if he so desired by deporting him to convict labour in Siberia. And through all the years of the reign the trade in "souls" continued, both in private sales and the public auction of serfs. Patrons of art among the seigneurs of the countryside maintained serf companies of actors or musicians, and a serf sent abroad to study stage design returned to Russia still a serf.

There could be no orderly transition from this state of affairs to a better and more humane scheme of society. The iniquity was plain, the moral revulsion already apparent. In 1790 Alexander Radishchev, a member of the nobility who had been educated abroad, pictured peasant poverty and the evils of serfdom in an eloquent little book bearing the innocent title of *A Journey from St. Petersburg to Moscow*. "Worse than Pugachev!" exclaimed Catherine in horror, and the sentence of death passed upon Radishchev, the proto-martyr of Russian literary radicalism, was commuted only to penal servitude for life in Siberia. A little later Nicholas Novikov, who once had found in the empress a contributor to his satirical journals and who had rendered no little educational service to the country as a book publisher, was sent to solitary confinement in Schlüsselburg for entertaining dangerous thoughts in his advocacy of the ideals of Freemasonry. The foundations of the literary censorship in Russia were firmly laid in these closing years of the reign; even Catherine's own Instruction now came under an official ban. . . .

III. INTERPRETATIONS OF ENLIGHTENED DESPOTISM

Based on Louis XIV, not Voltaire

CHARLES MORAZÉ

Charles Morazé (1913–   ) professor of history at the École Libre des Sciences Politiques, is a well-known contemporary French economic and social historian. Among his several works are an introduction to economic history and *Les Bourgeois Conquerants*, a study of the rise of the middle class. He approaches enlightened despotism by a study of its economic basis; this leads him to the conclusion that apparently enlightened policies were really initiated for the sake of increasing the royal power. He also shows how the despots borrowed from both France and England certain techniques which underwent striking changes in purpose when applied to backward central Europe.

THE WORK of the enlightened despots is usually presented as the application to government of the philosophical doctrines from the West, and particularly from France. The writings of French thinkers were supposed to be the source of the thoughts which guided the rulers of Prussia, Austria, and Russia in the transformation of the governments which they inherited. They were the forces which guided central Europe toward a new destiny.

We are certainly convinced of the capital importance of the philosophic ideas which enriched the eighteenth century. But we doubt, under the circumstances, that it played the role generally ascribed to in the development of enlightened despotism in central and eastern Europe.

The monarchs were concerned with their own trade. They were primarily interested in all the matters which arose from their own life and their work. They were submerged in the general questions which, day by day, they met in their work and which were framed in terms of the great economic and political movements of the eighteenth century. A poet admires a poet, a philosopher a philosopher. But the admiration of a sovereign tends, by the very conditions of his life, to go to another sovereign. The rulers took from France the example of Louis XIV and they meditated upon the reasons for his success. From England, they learned to create wealth.

While it is true that the enlightened despots displayed a lively taste for things of the mind, this was merely a personal intellectual attitude, and was little concerned with the diffusion of taste among their subjects. Joseph II was to pay . . . for his premature hopes of enlightening the masses. As for the other despots, they easily rationalized away the limitations to which they would not submit.

The work of the enlightened despots thus had striking effects upon the material level. They benefited from the experience

From Charles Morazé, "Finance et despotisme, essai sur les despotes éclairés." *Annales, Economies, Civilisations,* III (1948), pp. 279–282, 293–296. Reprinted by permission of Charles Morazé. Translated by the editor.

of France and England. They needed only to copy the attitudes which had brought the former to the summit of political power and the latter to the height of wealth. This imitation of a past which had proved itself occupied them more than the creation of the perfect world imagined by the eighteenth-century French *philosophes*.

Let us examine the case of Prussia. Frederick the Great intended to give substance to the idea that it was the duty of the prince to strengthen his state. Thus his first care was to provide himself with important financial resources, then gather under his control all the forces which might be useful to him.

The revenues of the Prussian king were drawn chiefly from his own domain farms. In each section of the realm these domains were farmed out to a bailiff who had to keep records of everything that was produced or expended. These accounts were submitted to a provincial board or college — the chamber of war, domains and finances. The presidents of these boards corresponded directly with the king. They were also responsible to the General Directory in Berlin, which included also the chief privy councillors and ministers. This General Directory held valuable cards — the complete records of the economy of the royal domains. It could bring about an increase in the rents for the farms, or lower them if bailiffs were hard to recruit. This extreme flexibility allowed them to give maximum service to the royal possessions.

This important source of income for the treasury, which was perhaps one-eighth of the royal income, was so well organized because . . . the king was all-powerful on his domains. In addition, in the towns the king received a service tax levied proportional to income from property and wages. While this tax produced little, the excise taxes charged on the sale of merchandise produced a great deal, a fifth of the royal revenue. These taxes appear to have been levied chiefly upon beverages. It seems that they were also reimbursed when the merchandise passed through the towns in transit. This flexibility which was so useful to commerce doubtless was due to the vigor with which the towns defended their economic interests. Finally, tolls and customs supplied an important revenue equal to about a third of the preceding taxes. . . . It was, in effect, based upon an agreement between tax collectors and merchants, who might otherwise have succumbed to the heavy real taxes which were especially notable in the Rhineland.

In the open countryside a contribution, or head tax was levied according to a system which had been perfected over several reigns and codified by Grumbkow. This revenue was important and about a third of the total, and was administered very wisely. The lands were registered in a list — a *cadastre* — which divided them into three categories, which were again divided into sections: good, mediocre and bad farmland; good and bad meadows; good, mediocre, and bad forest. The changes in land classification, which was very favorable for the treasury, were made by land clearing and improvement, which was encouraged by granting exemptions.

Only the head tax was subject to exemptions for those who served the king; others payed according to their state in life. But this was a tax of rather small yield.

To these old or reorganized tax rights was added a new resource, the salt tax. It was easy for Frederick William I to establish this, since all the salt in Prussia came from the mines of Hall and Unna in Westphalia. A minister of state had charge of them. There were also privileged salt mines in Pomerania, but these were forbidden to sell salt below the royal price. Frederick the Great took over all this organization and placed its administration under Frenchmen. Frenchmen also developed further the production and sale of tobacco which Frederick had reserved for himself in 1765.

The main part of the king's resources were of agricultural origin, just as in contemporary France, but the rulers of central Europe had the advantage of holding agriculture in their own hands. The king was the absolute ruler of a large part of the land and of his subjects. Moreover, he was their landlord. The less individual ownership of property developed, the stronger was the state. The doctrines favorable to individual property which developed in France and of which Voltaire was the notable champion, could only be disagreeable to Frederick the Great. On the other hand technical improvements which improved the productivity of the soil and the work of the agronomists enormously interested him because they contributed to enlarge his wealth. Thus Frederick busied himself with an Academy of Sciences, while dealing contemptuously with the *philosophes,* because the Academy at that time was really an Academy of Technology which enriched him.

At the same time he ordered villages and tenant farms which had disappeared to be reconstructed. He built new villages along the banks of the rivers which he had dammed, whose floods, so invigorating to the soil, had previously driven men from the land. He assisted the new settlers with lumber to build their homes, by helping them to acquire cattle, and by freeing them for a time from taxes and military service. Thus thousands of families were settled on the Netze and Warthe rivers, and soon the Oder and the Elbe, as well as the swamps of Magdeburg, Potsdam and Dromling, were the objects of the same solicitude. It is estimated that Frederick's intense activity after the Peace of Hubertusberg, in which he invested annually millions of ecus with no immediate return, resulted in the settlement of tens of thousands of families. And what he did himself he pledged certain landlords to do, especially in Pomerania, and he lent them money at low interest.

All this activity is explained by the fact that the king was the greatest landlord of the kingdom (he owned one-third of it). He intended to remain a landlord, and to benefit personally from all the advantages of the agricultural progress which he strove to promote.

This explains his attitude. He was like the landlord of an enormous farm run by his tenants. He secured for little or no expense the planting of alfalfa, clover and lupine, reimbursed those who planted useful trees (especially the mulberry) and purchased massive amounts of cattle. He was also acting like a landlord when he established immense storehouses of wheat everywhere which he filled in good years and emptied in times of scarcity, thereby establishing managed reserves.

True, on this point the good French *philosophes* began to look askance. These storehouses resembled monopoly terribly, and were opposed to the principle of free circulation of trade. While praised for his other activities, he was somewhat criticized in this matter. Moreover, did not these reserves also conceal disturbing military ambitions? This line of criticism sometimes went further. They reproached the king for failing to profit from his position as landlord of the realm to bring about a great redistribution of the land that would encourage small or middle-sized peasants. All the followers of Voltaire, for whom free property was the source of wealth, began to become indignant.

On the other hand, the more realistic Arthur Young had a better comprehension of Prussian policy. It was not the king's intention to create a better society but a strong state. This strong state supposed stocks of food supplies. That strong state required a full treasury, and the king earned more from his farms and bailiffs than he would have from developing small land holdings. Young also added that the individual peasant farmed the land less rationally. It was the bailiffs, hence the king, who benefited from enclosures, which Frederick the Great encouraged, along the lines of western technology but benefiting the state rather than the individual.

Thus enormous advantages were secured for the Prussian monarchy. It legislated like Louis XIV, but it had better possession of its lands and subjects. In France and England property rights had developed to the detriment of the sovereign's rights, but here they developed for the benefit of the state. The backward character of the eastern European economy was of great use to Frederick, because its development secured his power and not the growth of a new society.

This main consideration explains the strength of the Prussian army. The king had an armed force of 200,000 combatants, always ready to march. Half of his soldiers were the sons of peasants and day laborers who were trained intensively in the spring but then returned to cultivate the soil. . . . The other half was composed of foreigners, whose regiments were garrisoned in the towns. The troops only exercised their military functions twice a week. On other days they sought work and found it easily. Foreign soldiers could marry; they were encouraged to do so, become subjects, and settle in the country. . . . If they did not work on farms, the soldiers, especially foreigners, worked in the towns in industry. They thus appear to have been engaged in useful activity. The king could . . . militarize this activity. As master of the factories, he was able to direct them toward equipping the army.

Thus the king was led to take industry into his own hands as he had done to agriculture. Everywhere, especially at Berlin and Potsdam, Frederick the Great established factories which began to export. He gave them monetary advances and privileges. He established warehouses to store raw materials and negotiated trade agreements to secure foreign markets. His factories were rarely devoted to luxury goods, despite his efforts to develop silk and porcelain manufactures, which did not exist before his reign. What he desired most of all was to develop linen and cotton works, which were useful for uniforms. After the Seven Years War he furthered mining and ironworks. He was particularly interested in the Mark of Brandenburg and Silesia, despite the low yield of their mines and factories. The export of textiles, among other things, compensated for the king's need to import metals from other countries.

Thus, because he was the landlord of his kingdom, the King of Prussia had at his disposal an economy that was entirely at the service of the great idea of the reign: victorious wars. . . .

We should be under no illusions; no reform in Europe was due to the thought of the *philosophes*. Frederick II mocked Voltaire, Rousseau and the Physiocrats when he desired arsenals, filled his storehouses with grain or distributed cattle and seed. Catherine merely flirted with them, and the good Joseph who took their talk seriously was nearly led to his complete ruin. Nothing in the real or concrete institutions of Europe owed anything to the France of the eighteenth century; they owed almost everything to the France of the seventeenth century.

And the rest was from England. We have not discussed here in detail the machines of all kinds which filled the workshops and factories — they were often German but more frequently English. But above all (and it was a capital innovation for these countries which lacked mines of precious metals which had difficult or restricted connections with the Atlantic) they thought about England and its monetary system. State banks were established everywhere which gave the same kind of service to the sovereign as the Bank of England rendered to its government. All these rulers had a great advantage over the kings of England. They did not have, except in Austria, and there to a much lesser degree, a large and powerful political opinion to fear, which would be capable of discrediting their money, as . . . a way of expressing lack of credit in the sovereign. Russians believed in the bank note because they worshipped their Czar, while the English chose their king as a sign of the confidence which they placed in their money. The enlightened despots were thus more fortunate than Louis XIV in being able to create a monetary instrument before their countries attained the conditions which would have naturally given birth to it. They were thereby in advance of public opinion, and were able to use the financial instrument . . . against it.

The bank note was the vehicle of psychological forces. It was believed in because it had been believed in. It would continue to be believed in tomorrow although it served a policy which was detested, because it had been believed in previously on the word of a crown that was respected. Thus the enlightened despots accrued a store of confidence, in the form of money of a kind from which they could profit, and which would effectively serve them in the difficult years to follow.

How much more fortunate they were than Louis XIV! He might have created a bank and bank notes at the height of his reign and the adoration of his people would have accepted it. This would also have been true of Henry IV who thought of a bank, but was too unsophisticated and did not realize what a thing he was disdaining. The imprudent Regent, clever as he was, ruined everything by his blindness.

Thus, while the despots throughout the continent were accumulating treasure through the naive simplicity of their people . . . France gave manifest proof that a bank might be the worst instrument of royal arbitrariness. Instead of calling upon public opinion to support his designs, he antagonized it.

Thus while monarchies were consolidating themselves elsewhere, the French monarchy cut itself off from its economic roots, like an oak about to be felled. If France no longer gave to the world realistic models, but merely a veneer of ideas, it was because the body politic of the old monarchy was decaying from within and dying from lack of sap.

But was this thought always to remain a veneer? Were there not other institutions in France alongside of the vanishing monarchical body prepared to support a state with a different balance? And in Europe, would the other princes continue to mock this thought? Did they not have their own fields which in spite of them were preparing to bear fruit? If continental Europe remained at a stage where its political ideas derived more from the example of Louis XIV than from the thought of the eighteenth century, was that not a reason to think that the time would come when the French thought of the eighteenth century would be used for something more than preambles to proclamations?

This was one of the dramas of the western mind at the end of the eighteenth century, and reform was a completely integral part of the objective values of French philosophic thought. If French philosophy had been only a declaration, it would have been only the varnish with which Frederick, Catherine and Maria Theresa covered their own attitudes — just as the stylish furniture of the period was covered with varnish. The good Joseph was the victim of the ideas of the *philosophes* for having seen their solid virtues.

But possibly this philosophy would not have been fatal to Joseph had it not been applied too soon. Possibly it had destructive powers which Frederick and Maria Theresa had to be quick in deriding, because they soon would have no time left to do so.

But there was a second drama of the west. All the powers studied here resembled each other in many ways, the greatest being their imitation of Louis XIV. From England they borrowed techniques, but not methods of government. They inverted these techniques, one might say, by putting them to a very different use from the one which gave them birth across the channel. In England public opinion created the Bank of England and established its bank notes. In eastern Europe the bank note duped public opinion for the profit of a bank which was essentially nothing more than an extension of the royal treasury.

Thus a division was being prepared between continental Europe and maritime Europe; it was the old quarrel between the land and the sea.

A Compromise with Aristocracy

GEORGES LEFEBVRE

Georges Lefebvre (1874–1949) was the leading twentieth-century authority on the French Revolution. His careful analysis of the society of eighteenth-century France brought new insights into revolutionary studies and helped
reconcile conflicting schools of interpretation. Among his many publications,
two have been translated into English and read widely, his brief *Coming of the
French Revolution* and his extended history, *The French Revolution*. In this
selection, Lefebvre takes issue with the view that enlightened despotism was
a liberal movement. Like Morazé, Lefebvre judges it in negative terms and
points out that its success was largely dependent not so much on unbridled
monarchical authority as upon royal concessions to the aristocracy.

SEEN in historical perspective, the work
of these sovereigns appears to us to
mark the extension of western civilization
to the east. One aspect of this can be seen
in their work of creating the state, adopting rational methods of administration and
economy, and establishing modern armies.
Their originality consisted in the details of
adaptation, and also in the rapidity with
which the work was carried out. The latter was explained to some extent by their
copying of models slowly worked out by
the older monarchies.

It should be added that their efforts also
contributed to the diffusion of other elements of western civilization, to the establishment of an aristocratic cosmopolitanism
in which French language, literature, fash-
ion and art were predominant. In return,
the influence of rationalism, as reduced to
down-to-earth utilitarian principles by the
Enlightenment, assisted despotism, and
helped secure it [favorable] public opinion.
As in the West, rulers were led to ally
themselves with the bourgeoisie and encourage its growth by the need to obtain
officials for administration and economy
and the necessity of protecting and stimulating a nascent capitalism. As elsewhere,
"enlightened" despotism was an intermedi-
ate stage between arbitrary tyranny and
bourgeois monarchy.

The *philosophes* praised it without limit
for a long time. Concerned most of all
about intellectual freedom, they valued its
religious tolerance, the relative liberty accorded to philosophical thought, and the
patronage of scholarly research. Frederick
the Great, who wrote and conversed in
French, who shared their dislike for German culture and remained impervious to
religious sentiments, appeared to have enrolled under their banner. So did Catherine, especially when she drew up the
famous instructions for her reform commission. The Prussian civil servants and
Cameralists, the pastors, professors and literary writers were even more attracted,
since their sincerity was less restrained by
caution. Montesquieu and Voltaire would
have composed endless eulogies if they had
known of the law code which Carmer
drafted for Frederick the Great and submitted to his successor Frederick William
II. It proclaimed that the prince was subject to the law, assured individual liberty,

From Georges Lefebvre, "Le despotisme éclairé," *Annales Historique de la Revolution Française*, No.
114 (1949), pp. 97–111. Reprinted by permission of the Société des études Robespierristes. Translated by the editor.

62

and gave definite guarantees for the judges and other officials of state against arbitrary dismissal.

In reality, the humanitarian declarations of these rulers were hardly more than *jeux d'esprit*. They were essentially interested in the growth of their power, and they were careful to distinguish what could be of advantage to them from what was better forgotten. Joseph II, who was thought to act from intellectual conviction because of his zeal for emancipation, was particularly distrustful of the *philosophes;* having remained a good Catholic, he had no desire to meet Voltaire when he made his visit to France. As for Frederick and Catherine, public opinion was politically useful to them. Thwarted by the alliance of Austria and France, they did not disdain the praises of the *philosophes* which made that alliance unpopular.

It was the vanity and self-interest of the *philosophes* which made them lend themselves to such exploitation. Along with their pamphleteering passion, their efforts to indoctrinate the monarchs and to confound the clergy by contrasting the monarchs with the sovereigns of the East met with very moderate success. They did not stress the fact that for Frederick and Catherine, who were at a distance from Catholicism and who were the heads of state churches, tolerance was a much easier policy. Nor did they point out that it was the will for power and the natural and historical conditions, rather than the propaganda of *philosophes* or a concern for human progress, which govern the actions of rulers.

It is surprising that they did not even seem to have realized that the social policy of Frederick and Catherine was not one bit less conservative than that of the western rulers. Since the *philosophes* were only slightly interested in the peasants and the rabble of the towns, they were not disturbed that enlightened despotism profited these groups very little. The mercantilism of Frederick II, in particular, was aimed toward export trade, and not toward the domestic consumption of his people whose condition it hardly improved. In Prussia, poverty in the towns and beggars and vagabonds in the countryside were no less common than in France. They might at least have noticed the situation of the middle class. The latter were granted some concessions in return for their services, were given some subordinate posts, and were sometimes ennobled for exceptional service. They were formed into privileged corporations in the towns, freed from military service, and were able to acquire land and serfs. But the condition of the middle class still remained subordinate. In principle, ownership of land was the monopoly of the nobility, and it was nearly the same for the higher administrative offices and military command. No doubt, the most serious grievances were in economic matters. If the capitalist entrepreneur was benefited by protectionism, individual initiative was thereby stifled, and not only by regulations. In order to assure the collection of the excise tax in Prussia, the king forbade manufacture and trade outside the limits of the towns. In Russia the peasants were serfs of the crown or of the lords, and the middle classes could not employ them without permission. In the west, commercial capitalism was able to get control of the artisan class by means of exploiting the rural hand workers, who were underpaid and exempt from guild regulation. Much of what we call industry was merely the supervision which an urban merchant exercised over the domestic workers scattered through the villages. By impeding this development, the new monarchies obstructed the rise of the middle class, and at the same time endangered the success of their own economic work.

The enlightened despots conceived the social structure in the same way as their western rivals. The aristocracy seemed to them to be the class best suited to assist them. Peter the Great, by means of the *Chin* (a rigid system of rank based upon government service) tied the nobility to the service of the state, and Frederick the Great thought that his officers should normally come from the aristocracy. Though his predecessors, who were occupied with the subjection of the nobility, looked upon it with suspicion, he had confidence in it for it had become docile. He allowed the nobility to retain a degree of autonomy. The *Landrat* of the *Kreis* (the local county administrator) was a local nobleman nominated by his peers and confirmed by the king. Wherever parliamentary estates still remained, the nobles themselves governed. Frederick even aided the Junkers financially by organizing mutual mortgage loans in some provinces; it did not occur to him to offer the same advantages to the peasants.

Catherine II was inclined to be even more conciliatory. A German in origin, she knew that she was suspect because of her nationality. Everyone knew that the authority of the Czars was limited by the formation of aristocratic conspiracies and by royal assassination. She herself had set an example by dethroning her husband and either commanding or authorizing his death. While the German rulers, sure of their legitimacy, exercised their despotism with austerity and severity, she considered favoritism to be the guarantee of her security. But she also treated her nobility gently, and ended by issuing them a charter which formed them into special bodies within each province, with their assemblies and elected officials, and with their own special law courts. By such tacit compromise the enlightened despots secured the compliance and cooperation of the aristocracy. But the most characteristic feature of this agreement was that the peasants paid the price. . . .

Frederick II was quite convinced that the economists were right in demanding that the peasant be emancipated and transformed into a proprietor or a wage-worker, since the hope of gain would be infinitely more effective in stimulating hard and conscientious work than was coercion. He abolished serfdom on his own royal domain farms, authorized the fixing of rates for labor services, and even their reduction, as

well as that of ground-rents. But he did not dare to intervene in the economy of the noble estates. At most, in some provinces he directed that registers of land be drafted which would fix the peasants' obligations once and for all. But even here he was not completely obeyed. The Prussian state was more concerned about the practice of evicting peasant tenants (*Bauernlegen*) because it affected the tax yield and endangered the recruitment of soldiers. But it contented itself with restricting the practice and never fully took the situation in hand . . .

In Russia it was worse. The serf had no access to the state courts. He could be detached from his land, separated from his family, sold or deported. Once Catherine II curbed the tyranny of some lord who had tortured his serfs or put them to death. She did not repeat her action. She even gave away to her favorites large numbers of peasants from the royal domains, where they were supposedly better treated. Even worse, she introduced serfdom into the Ukraine after she conquered it.

Joseph II's contrary experience proved that compromise with the aristocracy was an essential condition for the success of enlightened despotism in Prussia and Russia. His administrative reforms suppressed the autonomy of the nobility by eliminating the provincial estates, and in Hungary particularly eliminating his cooperation with the *comitats* and the *tables* (local units of aristocratic self-government). He abolished serfdom both on the nobles' lands and on his own. In reorganizing the land tax, he dared to set a fixed limit on the percentage of the peasants' income which might be paid to the landlord. As a result, the feudal interests led the resistance which brought about his defeat, which was most strikingly symbolized in the abandonment of his financial reforms. In the course of the reaction which followed his death, his defeat was confirmed by the reestablishment of the nobility in its privileges.

Like the traditional policy of the western powers (at least those who did not lack practical intelligence) from which it did not substantially differ, the despotism of the enlightened sovereigns of the eighteenth century contained a contradiction: it stimulated the growth of the middle classes, and yet at the same time it was not fully successful except in alliance with the aristocracy, while it was conflict with the aristocracy which checked Joseph II and which forced Louis XVI to convene the Estates General. . . .

Enlightened Despotism and the French Revolution: Similar Goals, Different Methods

ERNST WALDER

A professor of history at the University of Bern, Ernst Walder (1914–) has done a number of historical studies on Swiss and German history from the sixteenth to the nineteenth century. He is the editor of the *Schweizer Beiträge zur allgemeine Geschichte.* The following portion of his article in that journal discusses the striking similarities between the goals of the enlightened despots Frederick the Great, Joseph II and Peter Leopold of Tuscany, and those of the French Revolutionary Assembly of 1789. He also suggests the evolution in the later phase of enlightened despotism from the rather conservative Frederick to the advanced theories of Leopold.

IN SEPTEMBER 1789 Joseph II's government in the Netherlands published and distributed a pamphlet which compared the reform policies of Josephine's enlightened absolutism with the revolutionary August decrees of the French National Assembly. Its title confirmed the similarity of the goals pursued: "The Truth, or a Comparative Table of the Changes planned by the Emperor and the Measures decreed by the National Assembly in France." This comparison was intended to make clear to the Belgian subjects, whose resistance to the political reforms of Joseph II took on new strength under the influence of revolutionary . . . France, that the representatives of the French people asked for nothing else but what the Emperor had long . . . sought to carry out in his territories. The armed uprising which followed a few weeks later in the Netherlands, in spite of the official explanations, only appeared to Joseph II as a proof of the irrationality of the people. . . . Joseph II maintained that the Brabanters revolted because he wanted to grant to them what the French nation demanded with loud cries.

The idea that enlightened absolutism and the French Revolution both strove for common goals was also held by upper and highest-level government officials in contemporary Prussia. The enlightened civil servants, who had been educated to government service under Frederick the Great, took what was by no means a negative attitude toward the revolution in the west. Their comments for the most part were in

From Ernst Walder, "Zwei Studien uber den aufgeklärten Absolutismus," *Schweizer Beiträge zur allgemeine Geschichte,* XV (1957), pp. 134–156. Reprinted by permission of Herbert Lang & Cie. of Bern and Ernst Walder. Translated and abridged by the editor.

agreement. They evaluated the French Revolution as an event which meant political progress for France, and saw in it the realization of basic principles which had also been applied to the Prussian State since the reforms of Frederick the Great. Here [in Prussia] they were already on the way toward accomplishment, and unlike France, they did not require the assistance of a revolution from beneath. . . .

In these contemporary pronouncements, in which enlightened absolutism expressed its relationship to the French Revolution, [there appear] . . . two forces working toward the same political goal, but seeking to reach it by different methods, the one from above by authoritarian decrees, the other from below with the aid of unchained popular force. . . . It was this idea of two revolutions which the majority of progressive or liberally minded Germans appear to have held, and this determined their uncertain attitude toward the disturbance in the West. Schlözer, the "Father of German liberalism," expressed it most clearly: the French Revolution was a necessity for France, where the government paid no heed to human rights and firmly rejected its own age . . . but "God preserve us Germans from a revolution carried out in the manner in which it occurred in France!" . . . Schlözer was convinced that the [German] governments could not in the long run escape the effect of an enlightenment pressed upon them continually from below. This was a belief the German Jacobins certainly did not share; they thought otherwise.

What was a question of political belief in the age of the French Revolution presents itself as a highly complex problem for the historian . . . as a basic problem of modern history, which will be here critically discussed. What was the relation, historically considered, of the French Revolution and enlightened absolutism to one another? . . . Joseph II has been called "the Revolutionary Emperor," the "Rebel in Purple." How must that be understood?

In what sense was enlightened absolutism revolutionary? What of the agreement in final goals which enlightened absolutism was supposed to have shared with the French Revolution . . . which they sought to reach by different paths with different methods? Out of the French Revolution arose the modern constitutional and republican state. Did the inner tendencies of enlightened absolutism either intentionally or unintentionally lead to this same goal? Otto Hintze and Leo Just appear to affirm the question, while Fritz Hartung denies it. What possibilities did enlightened absolutism have, what were its limits, what were its effects? . . .

By enlightened absolutism, we mean here the concrete absolute principality of the age of the Enlightenment — the second half of the eighteenth century — which was influenced by the intellectual movement of the Enlightenment and which was supported by it in its work of reforming, renewing and revising the inner conditions of the state. One of the chief areas of this enlightened absolutism was German central Europe — Prussia, Austria, and alongside them . . . smaller and middle sized states like Baden under Karl Friedrich or the Duchy of Saxe-Weimar under Karl August. It also appeared outside of Germany, with especially rich expression in Italy. . . .

I will attempt to limit my discussion of the relation between these two forces . . . to three main representatives of enlightened absolutist rule: Frederick the Great, Joseph II and Peter Leopold of Tuscany, who seem to me to embody the essential features of European enlightened absolutism. I begin with the question of the intellectual and ideological connections and similarities between enlightened absolutism and the French Revolution. Since the three princes mentioned acknowledged the outlook and basic principles of the European Enlightenment in their reform activities, and since the French Revolution, on its side, carried out the ideas and postulates of the Enlightenment, it seems [reasonable] to regard the movement of the Enlightenment as the common link. . . .

A few historians, especially the French, have pursued the trend of recent research which estimates the influence of enlightened ideas upon the government of the so-called enlightened despots as rather slight. They point out the continuity in the governing practices of absolutism and argue that there is no essential distinction, resulting from the influence of the Enlightenment, between the so-called enlightened absolutism and the preceding older absolutism. Charles Morazé goes the farthest in regarding the ideas which the enlightened despots took over from the French *philosophes* as only a pretty varnish. . . . It was not, [according to Morazé] so much the France of the eighteenth century as the seventeenth century which stimulated these rulers, and all followed the example of Louis XIV. . . . The Austrian Emperor was a special exception. The old master of French Revolutionary history, Georges Lefebvre, expressed himself similarly: governmental practice of the eighteenth century did not essentially differ from earlier practice. The humanitarian declarations of the enlightened monarchs were mere *jeux d'esprit*. The political attitudes of these princes was determined by the will for power, and the natural and historical situations which they found in their kingdoms, not by the propaganda of the *philosophes*.

Accordingly, the Enlightenment would be only of slight significance for enlightened absolutism. Such an attitude could only be understood, and with restrictions, could only be maintained if one looked one-sidedly at the movement of the so-called *philosophes* and economists in France—the Voltairians, Encyclopedists, Physiocrats, etc.—and the new viewpoints and plans for the happiness of mankind which they promoted. But alongside this French enlightenment, there were also other forms of enlightenment, especially the German. It was not simply a mere borrowing from or stereotype of the French but possessed its own special content and character. Its outlook and doctrines could and did affect the absolute principality in Germany. . . .

Much more important . . . the Enlightenment signified not only a total sum of new ideas of definite thought content, but beyond that also a new mode of thinking, a new intellectual attitude . . . which created a new intellectual climate in Europe by the wave of its new protestations, ideas, solutions and demands. One must seek out the enlightened in enlightened absolutism in this general "spirit of the enlightenment . . . ," not in the acceptance of particular physiocratic reform projects. . . . The rule of Frederick the Great, Joseph II and Peter Leopold would only have been possible in the spiritual climate of the enlightened eighteenth century, and would have been utterly inconceivable with Louis XIV. When, for example, Joseph II decreed . . . in 1787 that one would no longer kiss the hand or bend the knee before the All-highest Ruler, because such honors were incompatible with human dignity and were due to God alone, and when all three monarchs repeatedly stressed in their instructions for the education of princes that all men were equal and that they had been kneaded from the same dough as the others, that they could justify the special position that they enjoyed among their fellow men only by restless work for the well-being of their subjects — all this showed a conception of monarchy which was very alien to the older absolutism of Louis XIV, and which corresponded to the . . . thought of the Enlightenment.

This new conception of monarchy . . . was an aspect of what Fritz Hartung has called "the disenchantment of the Divine-right monarchy." And this disenchantment, in which the monarchs themselves cooperated, was part of a general process, the secularization of thought and life brought about by the Enlightenment. . . .

In contrast to the sacred conception of kingship, which was still effective in the age of Louis XIV, [monarchy] came to be understood as a purely secular and human institution. The downfall resulted from the victory of the natural law conception and origin of royal authority which the Enlightenment brought about. . . . Whoever accepted it, also accepted that proposition that the monarchy was an institution created by the people, derived from the people, that the exercise of sovereign powers was mandated by the people, that . . . authority was delegated from the people.

Frederick the Great and Peter Leopold expressly acknowledged this idea. In 1738, while still Crown Prince, Frederick in his "Considerations on the Present State of Europe" stated that the rank, the position for which the princes so zealously strove . . . was only the work of the people. They were endowed with their power from the people, had received their dignities from them, and therefore had to rule in a manner consonant with the intentions of their constituents. . . . Peter Leopold expressed himself in exactly the same way: the prince must always be aware that he is a man, that he owes his position only to the contract between other men, and that he had to fulfill all the duties and obligations which other men expected of him, in return for the privileges which they had granted him. . . . "I believe that the sovereign is only a delegate and representative of the people, albeit an hereditary one, and that he must dedicate to them all his labor and concern. I believe that the sovereign may rule only according to the laws and that his people are his constituents." Joseph II . . . also essentially conceived his authority in this sense. . . .

This touches very closely the political ideology of . . . the French Revolution, with its doctrine of popular sovereignty and the conclusion that legitimate laws are the expression of the popular will. If authority as conceived by Frederick the Great and Peter Leopold was derived from the people, and originated in . . . a popular social contract, this signified finally that the legal basis of authority was in the will of the people.

The deduction that not only a concern for the peoples' well-being, but also the peoples' will legitimized a sovereign was only drawn by one of the three enlightened despots, Peter Leopold. We have a whole series of projects and memoranda drawn up by himself and his colleagues between 1779–1782 for a constitution which would have transformed the enlightened absolute monarchy of the Grand Duchy of Tuscany into a parliamentary constitutional state. One of the memoranda expressly refers to the principle of popular sovereignty: "In all states, the sovereign power resides solely in the body of the nation, from which emanates all legitimate authority." The final constitutional draft . . . of 1782 described the government which was founded by the Medici . . . by force as being wholly arbitrary and unjust, since it was not based on the agreement of the people which alone could legitimize it. Peter Leopold desired to give back their natural freedom to all the subjects of Tuscany . . . by constitutionally refounding the state with their . . . participation and agreement. The last section of the preamble informs of the desire of the prince that the Grand Duchy be represented by a body of freely elected persons. . . . In 1790 Peter Leopold repeated in his political confession of faith that the ruler should strive for the people's well-being and happiness "not as he wanted to, but as they themselves wanted and felt," and that the people never would be able to abdicate their inalienable natural rights, or be deprived of them by unspoken or enforced consent.

The idea of an enlightened absolutism based on natural law and . . . incontestable human rights was hereby thought to its logical conclusion. The result would be the self-abolition of absolutism. But Peter Leopold only took this step in his mind, not in political reality. The Tuscan constitution was never put into force, despite the Grand Duke's expressed intention as late as 1790 — a few weeks before he left Tuscany to succeed Joseph II in Vienna — to put the finished document in effect.

The consequence toward which the enlightened absolutism of Peter Leopold had been led from its natural law foundations . . . could only be avoided if it was enlarged by the admission that the transfer of authority from the people to the prince . . . was unique, unlimited and irrevocable. Since Frederick the Great, like Joseph II, did not recognize the existence of inalienable and undeniable human rights in the area of politics, they were able to maintain their absolute principles. . . . For both princes it was certain that a ruler must carry out his duties as if he were liable at any moment to account to his fellow citizens. But they both denied the right of these fellow citizens to demand an accounting of the prince. . . .

This was no new ideology, but the older one of absolutism as it developed since the end of the middle ages, especially in France. [It maintained] that in relations with the particular interests of his provinces and classes, the prince upheld the general interest of the country. Placed above all the provinces, classes, corporations and private persons, he was the only one who could see the common good, and determine what the general welfare demanded.

All absolutists appealed to the common good, before whose command all particular interests . . . and special privileges must yield, even the enlightened absolutists. This also means that all absolutism, not merely enlightened absolutism, contained a revolutionary tendency which received a strengthened impulse from the Enlightenment, which added natural law and reason as further courts of appeal against historical, traditional rights. . . . In which direction did this revolutionary tendency point? Was it to the same goals which the French Revolution pursued?

The latter declared liberty, equality and fraternity as its motto. There is no doubt which of these the three mentioned representatives of enlightened absolutism had

in mind, when they spoke about common aims with the French Revolution.

The minister Struensee believed that he could predict a revolution from above for Prussia because the King, Frederick William III, was a democrat in his own way and worked continually for a limitation of the privileges of the nobility. By following Joseph II's plans, but only more slowly, in a few years there would be no more privileged classes in Prussia. When, on the other hand, Joseph II . . . could describe the constitution adopted by the [French] Estates General as a "plagiarism," "a large part of the things which I have already conceived and introduced for the common good," it could only apply to the destructive work of the National Assembly: the abolition of the feudal system, elimination of the privileged orders, and of the historic rights of provinces, districts, classes and persons, the end of special rights to taxation, ecclesiastical, civil and military offices. In other words, the establishment of equality with a single word; and in this Joseph II could readily recognize his own spirit. . . . The same efforts characterized the enlightened absolutism of his brother Peter Leopold.

Egalitarian, levelling, unifying tendencies were part of the whole general development of absolutism, not only enlightened absolutism. But it may be ascertained that the Enlightenment gave these policies a new impulse, a new foundation and a new justification. Joseph II, by adopting the idea of the natural equality of man as well as the individual way of thought of the Enlightenment, spoke not only of the "common good" mentioned by older absolutists, but also of the "good of the greatest number. . . ." One might remember that these words, with their reference to "the greatest number" as a chief argument against the privileged position of the nobility, may be found also in the pamphlet of the arch-apostle of the Revolution, the Abbé Sieyès, "What is the Third Estate?" . . . In so far as it remained true to itself, enlightened absolutism wanted equality, and prepared the path for it. Can that also be said about freedom, the other of the three values which the French Revolution had as its goal?

An Italian subject of Joseph II, and one of the greatest representatives of the Italian enlightenment, Count Pietro Verri asserted . . . in 1777 that civil liberty grew in proportion to the concentration of power in a single hand. This at first remarkable sounding position may be explained by Verri's second postulation, that a dictator was necessary to carry out reforms, not a senate. Verri and others who simultaneously affirmed freedom and enlightened absolutism in the enlightenment period wanted to see the prince endowed with absolute power in a negative sense, namely, to tear down.

[They desired] privileges to be abolished, old institutions to be destroyed, obstacles put out of the way, chains broken and authority unthroned; in a word the path made clear. That enlightened absolutism in this sense could and did have its effects is indisputable, but we recognize the limitations which were thereby set. Above all, one must ask for whom it made the path free and clear. The general welfare, the common good was named as the goal. But the common good according to Frederician and Josephine enlightened absolutism was only to be determined by the prince. . . . In 1789, when the French people arose against the old laws and the old powers, they put against this viewpoint the new idea that the people must take their fate into their own hands.

Enlightened Despotism and the French Revolution: Rejected, yet Fulfilled

GEORGES LEFEBVRE

ENLIGHTENED DESPOTISM has frequently been compared to the French Revolution in order to conclude that the brusque changes made by the latter were unnecessary and that the former might have achieved the same social results at a lesser cost. It follows from what has been previously said that such an assertion is equivocal.

If we think of the enlightened despotism of the *philosophes,* we can defend the assertion, on the grounds that they had persuaded the rulers to grant equality of rights at the expense of the aristocracy — though this must remain problematical, because no monarch actually attempted to do

so. If on the other hand we mean the enlightened despotism of the rulers, the assertion is sophistical because it fails to take into account the contradictions which we have pointed out.

The discussion becomes confused because the French Revolution in part of its work merely completed the unfinished work of the monarchy, which had not been able to overcome the resistance of the privileged. The revolutionary middle class completed the unification of the nation and achieved a national administrative organization. A rational division of the country enabled the establishment of uniform institutions. Privileges were suppressed and all

From Georges Lefebvre, "Le despotisme éclairé," *Annales Historique de la Revolution Française,* No. 114 (1949), pp. 112–115. Reprinted by permission of the Société des études Robespierristes. Translated by the editor.

Frenchmen made subject to the same law. In all this, enlightened despotism and the *philosophes* received credit, and the understanding between the monarchy and the middle class continued. It is not surprising that the Emperor Leopold II and the minister Herzberg made favorable comments on the decrees of the Constituent Assembly. If they had been able to benefit from them, their own power would have been increased. In this sense Tocqueville ventured to conclude that the Revolution strengthened despotism by removing the obstacles which had restricted the central government.

But the French Monarchy was also the advent of the middle class. Louis XVI became a constitutional monarch, subject to a national elected representative body. The central government itself was severely restricted by its grant of power to equally elected local and communal administrations. The enlightened despotism of the *philosophes* was thereby surpassed, although we might consider that since they favored the middle class, the triumph of the middle class was neither in contradiction with their intentions nor historical significance. But for the enlightened despotism of the rulers, the blow was mortal. It is not surprising that upon reflection they condemned and fought the Revolution.

This is not all. The Revolution had another side, one much more important to the majority of Frenchmen. On the night of August 4, 1789 equality of rights acquired a resounding fame. No doubt the middle class was satisfied with the legal principle, but the peasants were deaf to it, and the aristocracy had been abolished by the same laws. The nobility not only lost its privileges, but its social position and wealth were also attacked. Its losses were aggravated by the later sale of the property of the clergy and the *émigrés*. It is understandable that the crusade of the counterrevolution was more an aristocratic than a despotic one — the alliance between monarch and nobility was finally sealed from this point on.

It remained for Napoleon to teach the sovereigns of the continent how to exercise personal power under the cover of a constitution, and so to preserve for despotism all the benefits which the work of the Revolution provided. It also remained for him to remind the aristocracy that equality of rights did not prevent the nobility from retaining its favored position in the distribution of government office, or if need be, from reestablishing noble rank and entailed estates. In this matter the British aristocracy had long offered a lesson. The history of the nineteenth century shows that these examples were not without effect.

A Foundation of Nineteenth-Century Politics

LEO JUST

Leo Just (1901–   ) professor of history at Mainz University is a specialist in European political and religious history in the age of absolutism. He has written on enlightened absolutism, France and the Empire, and the western frontiers of the Holy Roman Empire. He is particularly expert in the history of the small Rhineland states in the eighteenth century. In the following selection, Just assesses the effects of the period of enlightened absolutism upon German history in the period after the French Revolution.

CLOSELY CONNECTED to the problem of enlightened absolutism was that of its significance for the future of Germany. Judgement [on the question] still centers upon Frederick the Great, especially in English writings. This can be explained by the fact that the German dictatorship of 1933 expressly claimed Frederick as its model, and saw in him the beginning of an [historical] line which also included Bismarck.

But if we disregard the political question here, it must be conceded that the absolutism of the eighteenth century took on a new form after 1763 and led towards the French Revolution, as Walder recently demonstrated. . . . Burckhardt saw the personal dictatorship of the king throughout the period from 1740–1780, but expressly emphasized the turning point of 1763. The Enlightenment in Germany included the entire educated middle class and the princely bureaucracy. It hoped that what was established in France by revolutionary means might come peacefully from above in Germany. Even as critical a journalist as August Ludwig Schlözer, who seized upon all the examples of despotism in the German states in order to pillory them fearlessly in his *Staatsanzeigen* could declare: "Where can be found more culti-vated sovereigns than amongst us? The enlightenment rises as in France from below, but it also meets on high with enlightenment."

It must also be conceded that if not Frederick the Great, certainly Emperor Joseph II embodied an enlightened absolutism of its own kind which was really unsuccessful. Despite its long after effects upon the nineteenth century, it was outmoded by the French Revolution. . . . As far as Germany is concerned, it seems proper to maintain . . . that there was a specially expressed form of enlightened absolutism, at least from 1763 on, and that this absolutism as a specifically German phenomenon lasted beyond the age of the Revolution and Napoleon at least down until 1848. . . .

If Hartung particularly warns against overestimating enlightened absolutism, that is certainly correct when limited to Prussia. At the same time, this means that Frederick the Great has been overrated in his significance for the German development. It is forgotten that Prussia was then a purely East German state with only a few western appendages. The other German princes are also seen too darkly in Frederick's shadow. Certainly his example had some effect, even if Goethe's words about a Frederician at-

From Leo Just, "Stufen und Formen des Absolutismus," *Historisches Jahrbuch*, CLXXX (1960), pp. 143–159. Reprinted by permission of Verlag Karl Alber. Translated by the editor.

titude are exaggerations. Alongside them are remarks of others like the Swabian Weiland . . . who said: "King Frederick is truly a great man, but God preserve us from the happiness of living under his rod or scepter." Frederick's influence sprang chiefly from his enlightened writings, and from the enlightened aspects of his system of government. While the limits and meaning of his influence still lack complete investigation, it is impossible to speak of eighteenth century Germany as "Prussianized." That would be a misinterpretation of the highly original way of life in the imperial territories before the French Revolution. The warm discussions about reform proposals, the slow development of public opinion, the reception of the Physiocrats' ideas in Baden while Frederick rejected them, the literary and artistic culture of the small princely courts and universities, all this was unique in Europe, and at best had parallels in the Italian states. . . .

Naturally, there were also examples of crass despotism in the German middle and small principalities of the eighteenth and early nineteenth century, for example in Wuerttemberg and Hesse. But they were unable to arrest the effect of the spirit of the age, which prepared the soil for the future. Let the Duke of Wuerttemberg imprison the poet Schubart in the *Hohenasperg,* as later Austrian despotism [put] the patriots of Milan in the *Spielberg.* Wuerttemberg became nevertheless with Baden the chief center of later liberalism. And if it has been said that the modern ideas of individual freedom and the rule of laws grew out of absolutism, this is true not only of the Prussia of King Frederick, but at least equally so of the other German states of the Enlightenment period.

Ludwig Hausser remarked . . . that the German princely ranks possessed such a number of worthy representatives as had not been seen in a long time. Out of the new attitude of benevolent, humane and unselfish princely rule an admirable school arose, in which everything was done for the people, nothing by the people. This brings us to the question of the continuity of the special German type of enlightened absolutism.

Hartung and others see the end of absolutism coming clearly with the idea of popular sovereignty in the French Revolution. They also reject the inclusion of the Napoleonic system. Mousnier at least indicates the end of absolutism in Prussia in 1848, Austria in 1861 and Russia in 1905. But Hartung denies the monarchs after the Congress of Vienna the character of absolutists, and sees only their counterrevolutionary tendencies. Mousnier uses the expression "late absolutism" but does not develop the theme further.

The restored monarchy of the Bourbons in France was limited by the constitution of the Charter [of 1814]. The history of Louis XVIII and Charles X demonstrates that despite a few occasional minor reverses, one can no longer speak here of absolutism in the strict sense.

But [how about] the states of Germany and Italy! True, the 1815 Act of the German Confederation envisaged estate-type constitutions. In a few German states like Saxe-Weimar, Nassau, Bavaria, Baden and Hesse-Darmstadt such constitutions were octroyed or negotiated. But by virtue of their very origins in the Napoleonic Confederation of the Rhine, these states were predestined to absolutism. In countless new portions of territory which had changed owners in the secularization of 1803, the remains of old feudal constitutional arrangements had to be fused together. In Bavaria a unified state, a so-called "Bavarian imperial unity" had to be created out of completely heterogeneous territories which were added to the old Electorate: the Franconian bishoprics of Wuerzburg and Bamberg, the Swabian ecclesiastical lands of Augsburg and Kempten, the formerly Prussian Ansbach and Bayreuth. Thereby the person of the monarch took on a great, even decisive role as the binding force. The apparent constitutionalism which was established in the states of the Confederation of the Rhine, even where it survived, in no way changed the fact that the actual form of government was bureaucratic enlightened absolutism. . . . The influence that Austria exercised through its minister Metternich upon the German Confederation was bureaucratic-absolutist. . . . Frequently we see Mousnier's suggested "Stage III," the absolute rule of minister dependent upon a king, but exercising influence upon him: Montgelas in Bavaria, Reitzenstein in Baden, Ibell in Nassau. . . . Where there existed estate-like parliaments, they served only as a brake upon absolute practice.

The two great powers Prussia and Austria did not even possess this "so-called constitutionalism" before 1848 and in the middle and smaller states of North Germany things first began to change only under the influence of the French Revolution of 1830. . . . What could be seen of liberal tendencies in the South German parliaments [and in Prussia] and in the *Staatslexicon* of Rotteck and Welcker derived completely from the age of the Enlightenment. Naturally, occasionally these efforts from below met with "enlightenment from above." How much was spoken about the liberal attitudes of the Bavarian Crown Prince and [later] King Ludwig I when [the chief minister] Montgelas was dismissed in 1817! Like many of his late absolutist colleagues, he certainly accomplished important and lasting achievements for his country which may be felt even today, especially in the areas of internal state government and education. In the latter, next to religious policies, the impulse of enlightened absolutism remained most strongly effective. But whatever good the ruler intended or did, it was often restricted and devalued by the governmental practice of the bureaucracy, with whom the subjects came most frequently in contact.

The often cited German spirit of [political] passivity should be less attributed to the Prussia of the eighteenth century than to the absolutism of the pre-1848 era. . . . Bavarian justice reserved the right to force political prisoners in the period of the Hambach festival in the early 1830's to kneel for mercy before a portrait of the king. Despite the persecution of political leaders in the twenties, and the decisive warfare against [the influences] of the July Revolution in Germany, the absolute bureaucracy was by no means merely reactionary and negative. On the contrary, there lived in it the striving for an authoritarian state of justice and welfare which kept the happiness of its subjects in sight and was convinced that its real goal was the education of mankind. Conze in his article on state and society before 1848 correctly describes this attitude as "an inheritance of enlightened absolutism."

. . . The deeper we penetrate into the individual and national expressions of historical phenomena like absolutism, the more general schemata and periodizations disappear. In Germany, absolutism did not end with Frederick II of Prussia, nor with the French Revolution. It lasted until at least as late as 1840, because here the princely state remained in existence as a result of the Napoleonic period. The [1813] treaty of Ried assured the continued existence of the Confederation of the Rhine states, assuring the continuation in the next decades of whatever had begun in the ending eighteenth century. In Germany, the late absolutist state did not stand in direct opposition to the nationalist conspiracy, as was the case in post-1815 Italy . . . In the Apennine peninsula, Metternich's restoration installed or reinstalled princes who were rejected as foreigners by awakening Italian national feeling. But the German rulers were, at least in part of their domains, of old native dynasties, and were regarded with love or at least respect. It should not be forgotten that from a biographical point of view, a whole number of German princes reigned continuously from the eighteenth century into the pre-1848 era, and that the same was true of countless of their bureaucrats. Whether one should apply to this delayed enlightened absolutism the title of "German Late

Absolutism" must be determined by further more exact comparative research.

The problem of evaluating absolutism, especially enlightened absolutism, with regard to the German development is more difficult than periodization. Jacob Burckhardt wrote in his lecture notes that Frederick the Great had demonstrated what could be done with a docile people. A passive subject population was naturally a main goal in efforts to form a state based on laws and a welfare state, and an obvious goal of all absolute princes. The long duration of absolutism in Germany certainly influenced the development of the national character; only very late did there appear that sense of independent responsibility for the state, that feeling which we are still struggling to strengthen today.

The Seed Plot of Liberalism

LEO GERSHOY

DEFINITIONS of enlightened despotism break against the profusion of its contradictory strivings and its incompatible realizations. Most clearly it was not a mere phase in the internal development of any particular country. It was a broad and complex European phenomenon, a distinctive stage in European historical evolution during the course of which enlightened despotism not only modified its ideals but redirected its objectives. While the century during its entire course moved away from the pattern woven out of the elements of absolutism, fiscalism, mercantilism, and cameralism, the enlightened despotism of post-1763 differs markedly from the earlier period when Prussia was its principal seat and Frederick II its shining exemplar. In its latter phase, less under the influence of Rousseau, whose political impact was slight until the Revolution, than under the prodigious influence of the Encyclopedists and the economists, it swept over all Europe. The Physiocratic credo, for all its contemporary emphasis upon "legal despotism," was itself a fertile seed-plot of middle-class liberalism. Consequently, the enlightened despots were different embodiments of the changing spirit of the age, as various as that spirit and their own historical heritage and as individual as their personalities.

In its most significant aspect the eighteenth century was the great testamentary executor of the English legacy of the preceding century. In political relations it took over the bases of obedience established by the "bloodless revolution" of 1688 and built upon them the democratic speculation of Rousseau and the utopians. While many of its spokesmen renounced their cosmopolitanism in favor of cultural nationalism, the century itself reached one climax in the storm of revolution. The religious beliefs of the age advanced from the prudential deism of the English rationalists to a more vital secular faith, even, among a minority of freethinkers, to atheistic materialism. The *philosophes* cut the cord binding ethics to revelation and made social utility the criterion of morality. They appropriated the great scientific conquests of the earlier age, and in an atmosphere where fear of the mysterious universe yielded increasingly to confidence in nature as a great benefactor, they revolutionized agricultural and industrial production, bestowing wealth and power on the middle

classes. Most important of all they elabo-
rated upon the dawning hopefulness that
the facts of progress and the new psychol-
ogy of human behavior and man's capacity
had engendered, and they created the ap-
pealing myth of human perfectibility.
"*Sapere aude!* Dare to use your own understanding! is thus the motto of the Enlightenment," proudly proclaimed Kant.

But this evolution was retarded by the
inertia of inherited relations and deflected
toward other goals by the play of hostile
outlooks. The strength of the *Herrenstaat*
was a powerful deterrent. The rule of caste
and the entrenched legal "estates" held back
the realization of the ideal of a nation of
citizens. Economic progress, and the social
reclassification that that progress entailed,
was slow in areas lacking in the fluid
wealth that came from world-wide trade.
Vast sectors of the Continent lay blacked
out under religious superstition and cultural darkness.

Even where the old internal relations
were least touched, the power relations of
states grew more competitive as the new
technology intensified and transformed the
dynastic rivalries into fiercer capitalist
competition. States were compelled to
strengthen their internal position, the
weaker merely to survive and the stronger
to be able to participate in the struggle
abroad. Whether to prepare for vigorous
participation abroad or to ward off the
menace of social disturbances at home, the
rulers more than ever before needed order,
tranquillity, and security. Translated into
terms of instruments, that meant greater
revenue; efficient administration; reliable
police; stable judicial procedures; sound
laws; larger armies and newer tactics and
strategy; skilled diplomacy; and not least,
a policy of social welfare. The whole content of enlightened despotism turned
therefore on the solutions given by the different states to their needs and aspirations.
It hinged on whether the ruler adjusted
his policy to satisfy the demands that were
demonstrably new or subordinated them
to the interests of older social groups and

kept the bases of public relations intact.
Though in some ultimate sense the decision may have been made by institutional
forces, the immediate role of individual
rulers or their leading ministers was of
paramount importance.

Much that our age holds dear was manifestly served by the triumph of an enlightened despotism whose ultimate ends were
realized through revolutionary means in
1789. Its deeply embedded humanist and
humanitarian liberalism was subsequently
fused with and "corrected" by the less ingenuous economic liberalism of nineteenth-
century free enterprise; but together they
eventuated in parliamentary democracy,
utilitarian ethics, classical economics, and
the Concert of Europe.

The English triumph over absolutism
was consolidated when the objectives of
the commercial oligarchy were served by
the governmental authority of the landed
interests. Enlightened despotism in France
culminated in the violent overthrow of the
old order and the painful establishment of
precedents for parliamentary, middle-class
constitutionalism. The French and the
English examples together remained during the following century the inspiration
and the criteria to which the secondary
states of western Europe — Spain, Portugal, Belgium, and Holland — constantly
referred. Catherine of Russia, on the other
hand, made the best of two worlds. She
strengthened the old bases and bequeathed
to nineteenth-century Russia its heritage of
autocracy, aristocracy, and orthodoxy. She
also linked Russia more firmly with the
west and widened the doors already ajar for
the entry of European liberalism. Joseph
of Austria died brokenhearted, convinced
of his failure. But his Caesarian absolutism
inflicted a galvanic shock on old traditions.
The repudiation of his methods did not
destroy his ideals, for these remained the
source of Austrian liberal and democratic
strivings.

The combination of enlightenment and
despotism also served other functions than
preparing for the ultimate triumph of lib-

eralism. Least enlightened was the Prussian embodiment of the mandates of the age. Measured in terms of progressive social aspirations it was a dismal failure. Frederick as ruler, distinguished from Frederick the emancipated intellectual aristocrat and cynic, faced the past. He was utterly sincere in regarding himself as the first servant of the state wherein his power was legitimized by the duties that he assumed. But his improvements were consecrated to buttressing an antiquated edifice. There is no evidence to warrant the conclusion that his militarized state, whatever its power and prestige abroad, bestowed benefits upon the aggregate whole. He continued the process of unification begun by his ancestors but only by perpetuating their conception of legal relations. His program of social welfare was grounded on a primary calculation to stimulate productive effort in order to augment the power of the state rather than increase the store of public welfare. Tested in terms of his own postulates of action Frederick did not succeed too well. Authoritarianism during his lifetime did little to alleviate inner rivalries and stresses. Its efficiency was won at the price of much corruption and still more coercion. And twenty years after his death the Frederician state collapsed ignominiously under the shock of the military disaster at Jena.

Authoritarian rule pursued its course, both under its beneficent guise as efficient Napoleonic Caesarism and in its more naked form as administrative, bureaucratic absolutism resting upon the loyalty of new financial and industrial interests joined with old landed and military groups. These two modern versions of the *Polizeistaat* also devoted themselves to serving the greatest happiness of the greatest number, but too often security was purchased at the sacrifice of liberty. The administration of justice and finances retained, especially in central and eastern Europe, more of the eighteenth-century ideal of orderly efficiency than it did of equality of incidence. The opening of careers to talents went together with an unparalleled concentration of economic power and the aggravation of social distress. The Concert of Europe was never entirely free from the threat of renewed strife. Public instruction became the appanage of secular national states that guarded their authority as jealously as had the ecclesiastical directors of instruction whom they superseded. The eighteenth-century fear of educating the masses above their station in life died a lingering death, while the decay of religious intolerance was accompanied by the slow rise of racial and nationalist hatreds. The triumph of deism was equaled by the sweep of fervid evangelical revivalism. Though the Enlightenment bequeathed to the future its confidence in reason, it also left a legacy of despair arising out of the philosophical conviction that whirl was king. Feeling increasingly displaced logic, and environmentalists were challenged by intuitionalists. The philosophy of the natural rights of man was already on the defensive against the doctrines of the historic rights of nations before the terror created by the Revolution put the seal of victory on the romantic reversion to traditionalism and irrationality.

SUGGESTIONS FOR ADDITIONAL READING

Students who wish to continue their investigation of enlightened despotism might extend their reading into several areas, both in the realm of political theory and political practice. It must be studied against the background of eighteenth-century civilization. Good general accounts of the period can be found in two volumes of the Langer "Rise of Modern Europe," series, W. L. Dorn, *Competition for Empire 1740–1763*, and Leo Gershoy, *From Despotism to Revolution 1763–1789* (Harper Torchbooks: 1963). Briefer, but enlightening is F. Manuel, *The Age of Reason* (Ithaca, 1951). See J. O. Lindsay, ed. *The New Cambridge History* Vol. VII (Cambridge, 1957) for a detailed survey of European institutions and ideas. There is a fine section by Franz Schnabel on enlightened despotism in the *Propyläen Weltgeschichte*, VI, *Das Zeitalter des Absolutismus* (Berlin, 1931). Also useful are P. Sagnac, *La fin de l'ancien régime et la révolution américaine*, vol. VII of the "Peuples et Civilisations" series (Paris, 1941) and R. Mousnier and E. Labrousse, *Le XVIIIe siècle, Histoire générale des civilisations* V (Paris, 1953). See also Leo Just, "Der aufgeklärte Absolutismus," in Just, *Handbuch der deutschen Geschichte* Vol. II (Constance, 1956).

The Dorn and Gershoy volumes above contain useful bibliographies as do the two volumes of *Clio, introduction aux études historiques, le XVIIIe siècle*, ed. by E. Preclin and V. L. Tapie (Paris, 1952). Detailed historical treatment of aspects of enlightened despotism must be searched out in the various national bibliographies such as: Germany: F. C. Dahlmann and G. Waitz, *Quellenkunde der deutschen Geschichte*, 2 v. (Leipzig, 1931–32), brought up to date by B. Gebhardt, *Handbuch der deutschen Geschichte*, v. II (Stuttgart, 1956); Austria: K. and M. Uhlirz, *Handbuch der Geschichte Österreichs und seiner Nachbarländer Bohmen und Ungarn* 2 v. (Graz, 1927–30, new edition in preparation); France: C. de Peloux, *Repertoire général des ouvrages modernes relatifs au XVIIIe siècle français 1715–1789* (Paris, 1926) and its *Supplement . . .* (Paris, 1927). Works relating to Italy may be found in F. Lemmi, *Il Risorgimento, guide bibliografiche* (Rome, 1926) and more recent works in E. Rota, *Questioni di storia del Risorgimento e dell'unita d'Italia* (Milan, 1951); Spain: B. Sánchez Alonso, *Fuentes de la historia española e hispano-americana*, 3 v. (Madrid, 1952). Major works on Russia may be located in R. Kerner, *Slavic Europe* (Cambridge, 1918). Other bibliographies and historical works dealing with the period may be found in the *American Historical Association's Guide to Historical Literature* (New York, 1961).

The development of the absolute state, perhaps the most significant development in Europe since the Renaissance, still lacks an adequate general history. Dorn, *Competition for Empire*, Chapter II offers a good introduction. Valuable are the collected essays of Otto Hintze, *Staat und Verfassung* (Leipzig, 1941) and H. Haus- herr, *Verwaltungseinheit und Ressorttren- nung von Ende des 17 bis zum Beginn des 19 Jahrhunderts* (Berlin, 1953). The role of the nobility has been traced in A. Good- win, *The European Nobility in the eight- eenth century* (London, 1955), and the political aims of the privileged classes in R. R. Palmer, *The Age of the Democratic Revolution*, v. I (Princeton, 1959). See the national guides for the many particular studies of absolutism. Leo Just's article "Stufen und Formen des Absolutismus" excerpted in this book gives a good bibli- ography of recent work. See also the re- port on absolutism by F. Hartung and R. Mousnier, "Quelques problèmes concer- nant la monarchie absolue," *International*

Committee of the Historical Sciences, X *Congress at Rome, Relazioni,* v. IV, 3–55 (Rome, 1955).

The political ideas of the Enlightenment have attracted continuing interest in recent years and there is a large literature on this subject, most of it centered upon France. A still useful introduction is P. Smith, *A History of Modern Culture:* v. II *The Enlightenment* (Collier Books; 1962). See W. Kingsley Martin, *French Liberal Thought in the Eighteenth Century* (Harper Torchbooks: 1963) and the spirited surveys of P. Hazard, *The European Mind* (New Haven, 1953) and *European Thought in the Eighteenth Century* (New Haven, 1954). Individual thinkers are outlined in G. Sabine, *A History of Political Theory* (New York, 1961). The small classic of Carl Becker, *The Heavenly City of the Eighteenth-Century Philosophers* (New Haven, 1955) should be read in conjunction with P. Gay's critical article in R. O. Rockwood, ed., *Carl Becker's Heavenly City Revisited* (Ithaca, 1958). A philosopher's treatment of the continental Enlightenment is Ernst Cassirer, *The Philosophy of the Enlightenment* (Princeton, 1951). A. Cobban, *In Search of Humanity* (London, 1960) stresses the English influence.

As for the chief thinkers, see H. N. Brailsford, *Voltaire* (New York, 1935) and P. Gay, *Voltaire's Politics: The Poet as Realist* (Princeton, 1959); A. Wilson, *Diderot* (New York, 1957); J. Oestreicher, *La pensée politique et économique de Diderot* (Vincennes, 1936); R. Shackleton, *Montesquieu: a Cultural Biography* (London, 1961); A. Cobban, *Rousseau and the Modern State* (London, 1934). A good recent summary is T. Bestermann, "Voltaire, Absolute Monarchy and the Enlightenment," *Studies on Voltaire and the Eighteenth Century,* XXXII (1965), 7–21. Writers of lesser talent contributed perhaps even more to the development of the ideas of enlightened despotism, especially the school of the Physiocrats in France and of the Cameralists in Germany. On

the former, see in addition to Gershoy's book excerpted in this collection, G. Weulersse, *Le mouvement physiocratique en France de 1756–1770,* 3 v. (Paris, 1910) and his briefer survey, *Les physiocrates* (Paris, 1930). A short English treatment is H. Higgs, *The Physiocrats* (new ed. London, 1952). See also H. Holldack, "Der Physiocratismus und die absolute Monarchie," *Historische Zeitschrift* CXLV (1931) 517–549. On the Cameralists, the summaries of their thought in A. Small, *The Cameralists* (Chicago, 1909) are best accompanied by an interpretive study like F. Hertz, *The Development of the German Public Mind* Vol. II *The Enlightenment* (London, 1962). See also R. Aris, *History of Political Thought in Germany 1789–1815* (New York, 1936) and the good sketch of the Austrian Cameralist Joseph Sonnenfels in R. A. Kann, *A Study in Austrian Intellectual History* (New York, 1960).

A comparison of theory with practice is a particularly useful way of studying enlightened despotism. A good brief introduction to the despots themselves is G. Bruun, *The Enlightened Despots* (New York, 1929). On Frederick the Great, see the standard biography by R. Koser, *Geschichte Friedrichs den Grossen* 4 v. (Berlin, 1925), and the good English language treatments by P. Gaxotte, *Frederick the Great* (New Haven, 1942); and G. P. Gooch, *Frederick the Great, the Ruler, the Writer, the Man* (New York, 1947) which quotes extensively from Frederick's own works. The Prussian king's statecraft is carefully analyzed in F. Meinecke's *Machiavellianism* (London, 1957). W. L. Dorn, "The Prussian Bureaucracy in the Eighteenth Century," *Political Science Quarterly,* XLVI (1931) 402–23, XLVII (1932) 75–94, 259–73, gives a good picture of enlightened despotism applied on the local bureaucratic level.

For Austria, see F. Valsecchi, *L'assolutismo illuminato in Austria e in Lombardia* 2 v. (Bologna, 1931–1934). Biographical studies of Maria Theresa and her son Joseph include: E. Guglia, *Maria Theresa* (Munich, 1917); H. Kretschmayr, *Maria Theresa* (Gotha, 1925); P. Mitranov, *Joseph II* (Vienna, 1932); F. Fejtö, *Un Habsbourg revolutionaire* (Paris, 1953) and E. Benedikt, *Joseph II* (Vienna, 1936). See also the English language biography by Saul K. Padover, *Joseph II the Revolutionary Emperor* (New York, 1934). Details may be studied in A. M. Link, *The Emancipation of the Austrian Peasant 1740–1788* (New York, 1949) and Sr. Mary Claire Goodwin's Fordham University dissertation, *The Papal Conflict with Josephinism* (New York, 1938). More thorough treatment of the latter theme is in F. Valjavec, *Der Josephinismus* (Munich, 1945) and the collected sources ed. by F. Maas, *Der Josephinismus,* 5 v. (Vienna, 1951–1961). G. P. Gooch, *Maria Theresa and other Studies* (New York, 1951) gives a good insight into the relations between the conservative mother and her impetuous son.

For Russia, in addition to such general national histories as Kluchevsky v. IV (New York, 1960) and Florinsky 2 v. (New York, 1953) see the biographical sketches by G. Thomson, *Catherine the Great* (London, 1947); G. P. Gooch, *Catherine the Great* (New York, 1954); and the popular study by Zoe Oldenbourg, *Catherine the Great* (New York, 1965). Rather hostile is another popular biography by Ian Grey, *Catherine the Great* (Philadelphia, 1960). *Documents of Catherine the Great,* ed. W. F. Reddaway (Cambridge, 1931) is also useful. See also A. Kizevetter, "Catherine II 1762–1796" in *Histoire de Russie* ed. Paul Miliukov (Paris, 1932) and the several articles by Georg Sacke: "Zur Charakteristik der gesetzgebende Kommission Katherinas II von Russland," *Archiv für Kulturgeschichte* XXI (1931), 166–191; and "Katherina II im Kampf um Thron und Selbstherrschaft," *ibid.* XXIII (1933), 191–216; "Adel und Bürgertum in den gesetzgebende Kommission Katherinas II von Russland," *Jahrbuch für die Geschichte Osteuropas,* III (1938), 408–417; and "Die gesetzgebende Kommission Katherinas II," *ibid.* Beiheft 2 (1940).

For the other parts of Europe where enlightened despotism flourished, see: Spain: R. Herr, *The Eighteenth-Century Revolution in Spain* (Princeton, 1958); J. Sarrailh, *L'Espagne eclairée de la seconde moitié du XVIIIe siècle* (Paris, 1954); R. Altimara, *Historia d'Espagna,* v. IV (Barcelona, 1935); L. Sanchez-Agusta, *El pensamiento político del despotismo ilustrado* (Madrid, 1953). Portugal: brief survey in C. E. Nowell, *A History of Portugal* (New York, 1952) and the popular biography by M. Cheke, *Dictator of Portugal: the Marquis de Pombal* (London, 1938). Italy: see the Vol. VII of *Storia d'Italia* by Valsecchi excerpted in this book. Also L. Salvatorelli, *A Concise History of Italy* (London, 1940) and E. Rota, *Le origini del Risorgimento 1700–1800* 2 v. (Milan, 1948); L. Bulferetti, *L'assolutismo illuminato in Italia* (Milan, 1944); A. Wandruzka, *Leopold II* 2 v. (Vienna, 1963–); H. Acton, *The Bourbons of Naples 1734–1825* (New York, 1956); Scandinavia is treated briefly in the chapters of both the old and the new *Cambridge Modern History.* See also C. Hallendorf and A. Schuck, *History of Sweden* (London, 1929) and R. N. Bain, *Gustavus III and his Contemporaries,* 2 vols. (London, 1894).

Finally, the essays on the application of enlightened despotism to the various European countries inspired by the International Committee may be found in the *Bulletin of the International Committee of the Historical Sciences,* I (1928), II (1930), V (1933), IX (1937), and X (1938).

DATE DUE